"Are you overwhelmed by all that's happe[ning] [in the world and unsure] of what to do about it? Like a good frien[d,] [this book] is inviting you to take a deep breath an[d] [....Becky] shares how small kindnesses can add up to a big difference and why it's enough to do what you can, wherever you are, for whoever God puts in front of you today. Whew."

"With a click of a button or a scroll with my finger, I can effortlessly access inhumane behavior topping the headlines of news sites and social media. While it can feel like we are drowning in an ocean of name-calling, bullying, and forsake-thy-neighboring, Becky reminds us how one simple drop of kindness can ripple into a tidal wave of difference. Becky's real, lived stories of kindness invite us to consistently drink from a fountain where our nourishment will overflow into the lives we touch daily. She reminds us that persistent kindness may not make the news, but it will make a difference."

"Want to change the world? Start by looking for ways to make a difference with the people in your path right in front of you—those you encounter at the store, at school drop-off, at church, in your neighborhood, or right in your own home. As Becky Keife so masterfully illustrates in this book, you don't have to be wealthy or famous or have a bunch of social media followers to impact someone's life. It's often the small and seemingly insignificant things that can mean the most! We can't individually change the world, but we can change an individual's world. This book will serve as a powerful guide to do just that!"

"If you're like me, when I look back on the most meaningful parts of my life, I recall the kindnesses extended to me in a time of deep grief or stress. Becky has crafted beautiful stories of kindness and compassion that will make you want to be the hands and feet of Jesus in a time when the world seems against each other. I was immediately softened and reminded that everyone is struggling and facing hardships in their own way. To be met with kindness in these moments is a great salve on our wounds and speaks to the gospel living in us. I hope you'll be both compelled and inspired by Becky's words too!"

Jami Nato, writer, entrepreneur, and plant killer

"Becky Keife's *The Simple Difference* will remind you that you already have all you need to make an impact in this world: the ability to choose kindness. It's a concept we learn in elementary school and teach our own children, yet once our lives become full, stressful, and complicated, we struggle to prioritize it ourselves. Becky's invitation is simple, yet profound: choose kindness daily and not one of your days will be wasted."

**Manda Carpenter**, author of *Space* and host of *A Longer Table* podcast

"Becky's transparent writing style and humorous personal stories made this a delightful call to repentance for me. We tend to treat people as they deserve, but she reminds us that Jesus calls us to treat each person as we want to be treated. With kindness. I found it terribly convicting and empowering . . . and hope you will too!"

**Bruce W. Martin**, author of *Desperate for Hope*

"With a tender heart and a curious mind, Becky gently asks us to remove the armor we've donned in place of extending kindness to our fellow humans. She reminds us of WHY this much-maligned virtue is so important, and how God uses it to gather His people through us. I am so grateful that we have a guide like Becky, rooted in love and compassion, to help us see how a simple difference can change the lives of people around us, as well as our own."

**Erin Moon**, host of the *Faith Adjacent* podcast, resident Bible scholar on *The Bible Binge* podcast, and author of *Every Broken Thing, O Heavy Lightness*, and *Memento Mori*

"This book made me cry happy tears in almost every chapter! Beautifully written from the heart, Becky gives us tangible tips to add more kindness to the world and points us back to the ultimate kind soul, Jesus."

**Maghon Taylor**, author of *Betty Confetti* and *Happy Hand Lettering* and founder of AllSheWroteNotes.com

*the*
# simple
# difference

## ALSO BY BECKY KEIFE

*No Better Mom for the Job : Parenting with Confidence (Even When You Don't Feel Cut Out for It)* (Bethany House)

*Courageous Kindness:*
*Live the Simple Difference Right Where You Are*

### (in)courage Book List

*Take Heart: 100 Devotions to*
*Seeing God When Life's Not Okay*

### Look for other Courageous Bible Studies from (in)courage:

*Courageous Simplicity:*
*Abide in the Simple Abundance of Jesus*

*Courageous Joy:*
*Delight in God through Every Season*

*Courageous Influence:*
*Embrace the Way God Made You for Impact*

*For more resources, visit incourage.me*

*the*

# simple
# difference

## HOW EVERY SMALL KINDNESS
## MAKES A BIG IMPACT

## becky keife

### Revell

*a division of Baker Publishing Group*
Grand Rapids, Michigan

Published by Revell
a division of Baker Publishing Group
PO Box 6287, Grand Rapids, MI 49516-6287
www.revellbooks.com

Printed in the United States of America

Library of Congress Cataloging-in-Publication Data
Names: Keife, Becky, author.
Title: The simple difference : how every small kindness makes a big impact / Becky Keife.
Description: Grand Rapids, Michigan : Revell, a division of Baker Publishing Group, [2021] | Includes bibliographical references.
Identifiers: LCCN 2021003830 | ISBN 9780800741303 (casebound) | ISBN 9780800738051 (paperback) | ISBN 9781493431847 (ebook)
Subjects: LCSH: Kindness—Religious aspects—Christianity. | Caring—Religious aspects—Christianity.
Classification: LCC BV4647.K5 K45 2021 | DDC 241/.4—dc23
LC record available at https://lccn.loc.gov/2021003830

21  22  23  24  25  26  27        7  6  5  4  3  2  1

*To Chris,*
*whose love and partnership is one of*
*God's great kindnesses in my life.*

# contents

# *introduction*

## BE THE BLESSING

Sometimes stories are the runways we need to get up to speed before an idea can take flight. This is a book about the big impact of small kindness. Before we dive into what *the simple difference* is, why it is a message I needed to write, and how it could be the launching pad you need to not only change your life but impact the entire beautiful, fractured, ordinary world around you—before we give those big ideas and lofty dreams wings—I want to tell you a story.

This is the story of the woman I didn't want to sit next to on an airplane—and the way an unexpected flight ignited a powerful spark.

The smell of coffee beans and cinnamon rolls wafted through the crowded terminal. Passengers congregated like impatient sardines near the gate, waiting for the airline employee to announce their boarding group. The flight was assigned seating, so I was happy to wait until the last minute to start breathing recycled air. I was thrilled to be heading to a writers' retreat, but flying is not my favorite. At best, I feel squeezed and queasy; at worst, clear the aisle 'cause I'm sprinting for the lavatory.

I was already starting to feel anticipatory nausea (it's a thing), and the loud shrieking nearby wasn't helping. I looked over and saw a mom and toddler in front of a vending machine. The little boy stomped his feet until his mom handed him a blue bag of Chips Ahoy.

*Cookies at 8:00 a.m. aren't going to help anyone!* I thought.

Immediately, a pang of conviction trumped my snap judgment. Surely I have not been above doling out sugary snacks to my own kids to buy myself a few minutes of peace and quiet.

*Lord, forgive me for being quick to judge. Please bless this mama with someone kind and loving to sit next to on the plane. Help her to see You in her day. Amen.*

The traveling sardines eventually filed down the jet bridge. I followed to 17E. It was a full flight, so I was surprised to find my entire row empty. As I shoved my backpack under the seat, I had a glorious vision: three hours of uninterrupted rest and productivity. With extra space, I'd be able to concentrate on finalizing my speaking notes for the retreat and then catch a little snooze. I'd land ready and refreshed for all God had planned! I adjusted the air vent and closed the shutter. Deep breath. This might actually be a great flight.

Then there they were. The little boy with cookie crumbs on his chin, crawling into the seat next to me. The mom settled in and took off her son's shoes. He wiggled and shrieked and wedged himself on the floor between the seats.

"I just want to apologize in advance," she said softly.

And I knew. I knew God was answering my prayer.

*Be the blessing.*

I took a deep breath.

"Don't even worry about it," I said. "I have three boys. I know contained spaces can be tough." She smiled weakly.

The flight attendant walked by, checking that seat belts and tray tables were secure. "Ma'am, his seat belt needs to be fastened."

"Come on, Jack. Time to buckle." She hoisted him off the floor and held up the blue straps. The boy arched his back and yelped loud enough to make heads turn. "You're okay. You're okay," she said in soothing tones and let the seat belt fall back in place, far from her son's waist. The rule follower in me cringed.

The next three hours were punctuated by screaming and squirming. When Jack's mom tried to get the toddler to rest in her lap, his feet kicked against my thigh. When the cartoon on her phone ended, when she offered the wrong snack, when he dropped his toy car for the fourteenth time, Jack wailed. His mom stayed calm.

"You're okay," she said.

"You're okay," he repeated.

Somewhere between the complimentary pretzels and the woman in front of us glaring back *again*, I struck up a conversation. Typical questions: How old is your son? Do you have other kids? Are you headed home or going on a trip? Jack just turned three and had two older stepsiblings. They were on their way home to Dallas.

"It's not easy flying with a little one," I said. "You're doing a really great job."

"Thanks. This is way better than last time."

I saw a wince of remembrance flash over her face.

"Jack got diagnosed with autism a couple months ago. He's not very verbal and gets easily frustrated. But he started therapy, and it's really helping."

I had hoped this flight would be a quiet space for me to work and rest. That didn't happen. I didn't get to prepare for my meetings or take a nap. But I did catch a glimpse of Jesus.

When the seat belt sign dinged on, the flight attendant was quick to check my seatmate's status. Again, the travel-weary mother tried to comply. Again, Jack refused. But never once did this mama get mad.

Never once did she shame her child or try to justify his behavior. She just loved him.

Before we landed, I leaned over and said, "I just have to tell you, you're a really wonderful mom. You've been incredibly patient and kind in a situation that I'm sure isn't easy to handle. He's lucky to have you."

"Thanks," she said. "I wasn't always like this. But I learned quickly that I can make it worse or help him as best I can. He's a good boy, even when it's hard."

The engines hummed louder as we made our final descent. Jack nuzzled closer to his mama. With a stranger's tiny toes pressed against me, all I could think was: What if we're supposed to *be* the answer to our prayer? What if we changed the way we prayed?

Instead of, *Lord, bless them—Lord, prepare me to be a blessing.*

Instead of, *Lord, show them kindness—Lord, empower me to be kind.*

Instead of, *Lord, provide—Lord, give me eyes to see and a willingness to give.*

I deboarded the plane and was grateful for room to stretch my legs. Just beyond the gate I passed a vending machine with a row of bright blue-packaged cookies. I looked back over my shoulder and caught a glimpse of Jack. I mulled over the truth like a student rehearsing exam facts she doesn't want to forget: *Appearances never tell the whole story. Appearances never tell the whole story. Be the blessing. Be the blessing.*

Three years later and I'm still rehashing this story in my mind. I don't know if Jack's mom felt as marked by our thirteen hundred shared air miles as I did. I don't know if she thinks back on our flight with fondness for the lady by the window who didn't act irritated. But I know that I will always remember that day with gratitude for the way it flipped a switch in my heart. How it altered my awareness and my purpose.

Bearing witness to a woman's kindness to her son changed me. Choosing love and patience for the good of two strangers changed me.

She and I could have so easily made different decisions. Speaking for myself, it would have been easy to put in earbuds and blast George Winston in a forced attempt to focus on my work or relax. I could have reacted to each of Jack's shrieks or made it known that he was invading my personal space. (I know how to give a powerful stink eye and employ exaggerated twitches every time I'm bumped.) That would have been my natural tendency—sad as it is to admit. But moving beyond my normal preference to an intentional, others-centered perspective reshaped those hours up in the sky.

*Be* the answer to my prayer for kindness. *Be* the one who sees a stranger through God's eyes of love and compassion instead of my own judgment and inconvenience. It was only Jesus in me that prompted me to get off the high horse of my own annoyance in the airport terminal and even think to pause in prayer for this struggling mama-son pair. I'm so grateful the Lord gave His Spirit to whisper to mine.

But it's not enough just to hear. Our faith grows legs for change when we turn that hearing into doing.

The small shift from self-focused to others-focused, from perception to action, is the beginning of the simple difference.

The thing about love and kindness, or the lack thereof, is that we can rarely (maybe never fully) grasp its impact. I'm sure each of us can recall the heart-swelling care we felt when someone really saw us, when we received an unexpected kind word or gesture at just the time we needed it. I have saved voice mails and texts from friends when their messages were well-timed lifelines of affirmation and assurance. I digest their encouragement like long-lasting soul nourishment. Those things mark us. On the flip side, you can likely remember with sharp clarity a stinging, jarring, painful word, look, or encounter, be it from a friend or stranger. We deeply internalize the harsh, the damaging. Wounds of unkindness and injustice—they add up. They also mark us.

Through the gift of flying next to Jack and his mom, I saw with fresh eyes how our lives are made up of millions of moments stitched together with countless opportunities to decide what kind of mark we're going to leave.

At the airport, dry cleaners, doctor's office, or school pickup; where you worship, work, walk, and shop; when you're coming and going, when you're waiting and complaining; whether you're dancing in the rain or limping through the desert, on a dusty country road or a slick city street—in all places at all times, you and I have a choice: What kind of difference are we going to make?

Are we going to go through life on the autopilot of our own convenience and personal preference? Or will we learn to live eyes wide open to the individual beauty and needs of the people around us? Are we willing to make our daily errands and agendas an ongoing opportunity to live soft and surrendered to the Holy Spirit's leading?

This isn't about totally changing the course of our lives; it's about letting God change us and work through us in the very midst of our ordinary days. To say, *As I go on my way, Lord, have Your way with me.*

That flight from LAX to DFW is just one small glimpse of what intentional kindness looks like. I share it not to toot my own horn but to illustrate the kind of opportunities we all have to choose kindness on any given Thursday. Throughout this book we're going to examine a plethora of examples—not so we can create a mountain of goodness to climb or add more obligations to our crowded to-do list or heap on the weight of added expectations we can't carry. No.

This isn't a book that's going to tell you to do more. This is a book that's going to help you to *see.*

Question-asking is often the beginning of seeing.

We discover this nowhere more clearly than in the passage of Scripture known as the parable of the good Samaritan. We'll unpack this more later, but the primary question reverberates throughout the centuries: "Which of the three became a neighbor?"[1] It's a question-shaped shovel that digs to the heart of who was willing to see and respond.

I have a whole lot of questions of my own these days. I've got a hunch I'm not the only one. Questions like: In a world marked by division, how do we respect our differences and live in harmony? In a culture that praises likes and follows yet fosters isolation, how do we cultivate meaningful connections? When despair runs rampant, is real hope possible? When competition is elevated, is compassion still relevant? And at the end of the day, can one person really make any difference at all?

What if the answer to these big, complex questions had roots in a small, simple movement? I believe it does. It's called *the simple difference*—living the big impact of small kindness.

Turn on the evening news or spend fifteen minutes on Facebook and it's easy to feel like there is a war on humanity and everybody's losing. From divisive politics to strained race relations, school violence to mental illness, poverty and homelessness and cultural hopelessness. When the blue glow looks bleak, it's easy to keep on scrolling. It's easy to feel like the world is in a downward spiral and there's nothing we can do to change it, so why not just keep a low profile in our own protective bubbles. Bubbles that keep our heads to the ground and lives to the grind and don't make space for saying yes to being a neighbor. But when injustice gets too loud or unkindness hits too close to home, what will we do? Where will we go? When will we stop name-calling and complaining and start being part of the life-marking and change-making?

I get a little passionate, a little heated up because I care so much. But you've got to know this isn't a book about economic strategy, social divides, or political lines. We're not going to solve the world's

17

problems—or perhaps even agree on what they are—in the span of two hundred pages. What I do believe is that through this book we can come to agree that every life counts, and the currency of our small kindness adds up to a big impact.

I hope we will make individual commitments to live out the greatest commandment and the second one like it: "Love the Lord your God with all your heart and with all your soul and with all your mind." And "Love your neighbor as yourself."[2] As we learn to love in ways we never before contemplated or considered, starting in our own homes and neighborhoods, our personal pledges have the capacity to create collective momentum.

Imagine every person tosses a stone of kindness into their personal pond of influence, creating a ripple. My pond will be different than your pond, which will be different from the one belonging to the woman on Instagram and the guy across town. But what if every person in your family or at your church or on the planet cast a stone into their pond. Eventually the ripples would overlap. And like a tidal wave of kindness sweeping over our communities—the landscape of lives will be changed in its wake.

*The simple difference. The simple difference.* Hear the rhythm of the waves lapping up on the shore of your heart. *Every small kindness makes a big impact.*

At this point your heart might be swelling with emotion; maybe you're nodding your head, saying, "Yes! I'm in! I want to make a difference!" But perhaps you're also thinking, "Cut the hyperbole, Becky. Is this just a lot of hype? Another do-good bandwagon looking for a crowd to hop on before the wheels pop off?"

Please know that I hear you. I'm a flipping coin of passionate optimism and healthy skepticism because nobody's got time for a fad or phase without hope of real truth or change.

If you're not already a believer in the power of small kindness, I probably can't convince you of it in one opening introduction. But I hope to pique your interest enough to make you want to say yes to this invitation to learn more about the simple difference. Say yes knowing that you go with a guide, a fellow journeyer, who has grappled with similar questions as you have.

Over and over I've asked: When the problems are so deep and wide, what can one person really do?

Through my wrestling and Bible searching, through story collecting and my own simple difference living, I've still got a lot of questions. But I'm completely sure of this: our small, sometimes barely perceptible acts of love, kindness, and encouragement can not only put a little ripple in the currents of hate and blame, loneliness and hopelessness, they are enough to actually change the tide. When people live out the simple difference, it ushers in wave upon crashing wave of humility, mercy, and grace until the faces and culture they touch no longer look the same.

Living the big impact of small kindness is how we mark the world with love in Jesus's name.

God will call some people to massive platforms and shiny stages. He will send some to remote locations in distant places. We can cheer on the big-name influencers and overseas missionaries. We can (and should) pray for their clout and ministries and everything the "professionals" do to affect the world for kingdom good. But there's an urgent news flash we all need to hear: influence isn't reserved for people with X number of bank account dollars or Instagram followers. Impact isn't retained as a reward for those with certain letters behind their names or organizations headlining their fame. Most of us are called to classrooms or boardrooms, hospital rooms, washrooms, or LEGO-scattered living rooms. Our location and job description do not dictate our capacity for impact.

We are *all* born to be difference makers. There are endless opportunities to influence our families, churches, neighborhoods, and communities just by going about our daily lives. A kind word, a helping hand, a sincere prayer—these really are the little things that can make a big difference to the person you're face-to-face with.

The simple difference says, *I will put on a posture of kindness. I will look for ordinary ways to be the blessing in someone's day. I will notice others, encourage generously, and serve joyfully out of the abundance of God's loving grace.*

But please don't mistake simple for surface. We're going to dive deep into exactly what all these nice-sounding words mean.

Are you with me?

I'm imagining it already . . . a global family of simple difference makers.

What if every traveler were quick to extend kindness to their fellow seatmate? What if every neighbor were ready to fill in the gap of assumptions with grace instead of judgment? What if every boss and coworker and grocery store shopper went out of their way to meet the needs of others? Let's infiltrate every school and workplace, every subway and bus stop and yogurt shop. The world will start to wonder who we are.

They will soon come to know us by our mark—ordinary, consistent, extravagant kindness.

# *one*

# why kindness

I grew up in the eighties, when Mister Rogers wasn't old-school, as my kids would say; he *was* school! Daily I'd sit captivated by the friendly man whose smile radiated through the square box in my living room. I was eager to escape to a world of make-believe via a bright red trolley while learning about things like sharing and caring, dealing with angry feelings, and the importance of practicing. The "It's a Beautiful Day in the Neighborhood" theme song became a soundtrack of my childhood. As dear Mister Rogers exchanged his suit coat for a cardigan and his dress shoes for sneakers, I waited expectantly for his ultimate singsong question: "Please, won't you be my neighbor?" My preschooler heart was forever ready with a resounding yes!

There have been books written and movies scripted about the amazing life and legacy of Fred Rogers. Don't be surprised if a few of his sage words make it into these pages. But the thing about the Mister Rogers phenomenon that struck my childhood delight more than thirty years ago is the same thing that is still resonating in my heart today: it feels good to be wanted. It is a powerful thing to be seen—to belong.

That simple question, Won't you be my neighbor? is more than the ending of a catchy children's song. It's a declaration of acknowledgment, an invitation of acceptance. Mister Rogers wanted a neighbor just like you and me because he saw deep value in every person. "As human beings, our job in life is to help people realize how rare and valuable each one of us really is, that each of us has something that no one else has—or ever will have—something inside that is unique to all time," Rogers explained.[1]

As much as I love being on the receiving end of the unconditional acceptance the famous PBS children's program host offered his viewers, I feel compelled to ask the uncomfortable question: Am I really willing to offer unconditional acceptance in return? Can I say with Fred's same sincerity, "Please, won't you be my neighbor?" Can I say it to every person my life intertwines with or touches? Am I ready to be a neighbor to anyone my sleeve brushes?

Honestly? Not yet. But I want to. I believe that's what we're called to.

As we begin this simple difference journey, I'd like to hold up a question for us to examine: Why does kindness matter?

Put it in your palm. Stretch your arm way out and look at it. Turn it over. Pop the question into your mouth. Put it in your mind. Roll it around. *Why does kindness matter?* It's the question we've got to answer because if kindness doesn't matter then there's no point in pursuing a life that is shaped by it.

There have been many people who have made an indelible mark on the world with their kindness. Certainly Fred Rogers comes to mind, along with Mother Theresa, Princess Diana, and Corrie ten Boom. Perhaps you think of Nelson Mandela, who ended apartheid in South Africa, or Mahatma Gandhi, who changed the world through nonviolent resistance. Maybe if you know the name Jonas Salk you'd put him on a kindness pedestal for saving millions of children with his development of a successful polio vaccine, which he chose not to patent in order to increase accessibility (by default forfeiting billions in patent revenue).[2] Each one of these historical figures made an impact on society. But the question of why kindness matters cannot hinge on their examples.

It's not enough to pattern our lives after good people.

Why? Because the expression of authentic, love-driven kindness *will* look different for each of us. The unique people we will meet and the personal and varied circumstances that stitch our days together make the simple difference a one-of-a-kind journey. If we try to copycat the life and legacy of another, we're going to fall short.

I'm not meant to be a pioneer in children's television or a nun who cares for the dying or a secret smuggler of hunted Jews. Chances are these things aren't part of your life trajectory either. In addition to their *means* of impacting the world, each person's *motives* are likely to be equally as varied: expand access to early childhood development resources, ease the suffering of the hurting, save innocent lives, dismantle systemic racism, and on and on. We can all probably agree these pursuits are valuable! But we might not all be called, compelled, or equipped to give our lives to their mission.

Can we learn about kindness from the lives of remarkable men and women? Absolutely. We can identify common character traits and behaviors, like compassion, generosity, perseverance, sacrifice, and creativity. But we can't replicate how small, daily, on-your-way acts of intentional kindness look in someone else's life.

I can only show up to my life. You can only show up to yours.

(Not to mention the fact that even great people—remarkable and compassionate world-changing kinds of people—are still imperfect, and not everything about their lives ought to be held as the standard of excellence and imitation.)

So we can see how it's problematic to hold up a particular person as the defining reason of why kindness matters and make them our guiding example of how to live it. Well, there is one exception. One person we can and should turn our attention to who is both the answer and the model.

His name is Jesus.

• • •

Jesus Christ. God's only Son. Fully God who humbled Himself to live concurrently as fully man. Jesus, a carpenter who bled, a friend who wept, a leader and preacher and healer, and ultimately our Savior-Redeemer. Yeah, *He's* the only infallible standard. He's the *why* we can hang our simple difference journey on with assurance.

But if you don't know Jesus, if you doubt that the description I just gave is true, if you wanted a book about changing the world through kindness but didn't realize it was going to be steeped in all this Jesus-Bible-God talk, *please do not tune out or close this book.* I implore you to keep reading. Your questions and personal perspective are welcome here. Jesus wasn't afraid of skepticism and neither am I. Perhaps in your pursuit of a life of kindness, which is a commendable endeavor, you'll discover a kindness more real and radical than you ever thought possible—a kindness available to you through a relationship. I sure hope you do. Either way, there are stories in the pages ahead that are sure to make you think, infuse hope in your heart, and encourage you to live this one precious life well. So keep reading.

Now, back to Jesus. Born of a flesh-and-blood mother, the God-child who lived a sinless life and surrendered to a brutal death in order to pay off the incalculable debt of my sins and yours and every person who ever breathed an earthly breath—Jesus—is the epitome of God's kindness. This is where we must start.

Here's the broad stroke, bird's-eye view of the story of humanity, which is essential to knowing why kindness matters. (Hang with me. This will be worth it.)

God created man and woman. Upon Satan's twisted words and tempting, the man and woman chose to disobey God and ate from the tree of the knowledge of good and evil. Sin entered the world. Thus, an impassable gap became wedged between God and people. Their perfect peace, unity, and intimacy was forever broken. Shame and pain, toil and strife rushed onto the scene and wouldn't leave. This could have been the end of the story.

But God.

But God loved what He made, for He carefully and purposefully formed the first man and woman in His image. He breathed His own breath into their lungs and imprinted His likeness on the soul and sinew and every DNA strand of every person born since. God didn't want to remain separate from His creation. Love compelled Him to bridge that impassable gap of self-serving disobedience and brokenness called sin. For several generations, a temporary bridge called the Law was used. It was constructed with boards that looked like endless rules and sacrifices with limited and short-lived power. In many ways, the Law was less like a wooden bridge and more like a wobbly tightrope—few had the courage or stamina to cross it. Most jumped off while tiptoeing along because another way looked easier. And only a restricted group of people was even allowed access to this narrow and difficult bridge of redemption. The Israelites alone were God's chosen people who were invited to remain tethered to their Creator—and even they strayed from His love and protection (again and again and again). This wasn't enough for God.

God wanted to restore His relationship with *all* people.

So He offered a new bridge. One that would forever fill the gap created by sin. One that wouldn't crumble when a person fell short of upholding the Law. One that wouldn't need to be reconstructed over and over with flawless lambs on an altar or good works offered. One that wouldn't shatter under the weight of unbelief. This bridge was to be hewn from an unbreakable material. This bridge was the shape of a cross with Jesus stretched palm to palm across it. Nails were driven into the flesh of His hands and bones of His feet, sealing the purpose of the bridge with His pain. It's a graphic picture, I know. It should make our stomachs turn and souls ache. Strange as it may sound, this gruesome sight is also the breathtaking beauty of God's kindness.

If you know this story well, keep reading like it's a fresh revelation. We need to hold this truth with renewed awe and reverence. Let it mark you and unmake you and rebirth you. If this is like a foreign language, take a deep breath. Don't worry if you feel out of your element or in over your head. Ask God for eyes to see and ears to hear. He's got something for you here. We'll walk it out together.

The gospel story I recounted above is the radical kindness of God.

It's God's loving-kindness that He allowed Jesus—His beloved Son—to bleed red till the last breath left His heaving chest so that the red of our debt could be wiped clean. Jesus died so that you and I could live free.

I'm a mom of three boys, and I can't even fathom for one split second sacrificing a son for the freedom of others. I'm also a woman who has missed the mark more times than I can count. I've lied and cheated and coveted what someone else had. I've given my heart to pride, lust, and greed. I've torn others down to build myself up. I've purposefully disobeyed God because I thought I knew better. In other words, I'm a sinner. Our stories may be different, but I know sin is somewhere a part of yours too.

Our lives are like an overdrawn account with line after line after line of crimson debt too long and deep to ever pay our way out. The withdrawals of poor choices and bad attitudes, not-so-white lies, and justified deceit keep piling up faster than any good deeds can try to cancel them out. Add bitterness, unforgiveness, gossip, and unchecked anger to the ledger. Yet somehow the account is miraculously PAID IN FULL. We didn't do anything to earn this cancellation of our debt. It was a gift. From our heavenly Father.

This is what God's voice sounds like in the middle of our sin. Lean in and listen. These words are for you.

*I see you're weighed down. Let Me unload the burden. I see you're flailing and feel like you're drowning. Here's a lifeline that will never slip away. Just grab hold of My hand. I've made a way for you. You're no longer shackled by debt. You can breathe. And don't worry about paying Me back or losing this gift. You can't. It's yours forever. Because I love you and I want to spend today and eternity free and with you.*

(Take a breath. Pause. Respond.)

You should know that I have tried to earn my way out of spiritual debt. I've tried to be good enough, moral enough, successful enough, even kind enough to make up for all the yuck in my life. With slick words and sleek curves, with people's approval and impressive accolades, I've tried to fill the gap in my soul that keeps me separated from God. We weren't meant to be separate. We were meant to be connected. We were meant to be loved. And we are.

The reason my little-girl heart awakened to Mister Rogers's song is because I was and am wired to be unconditionally wanted and welcomed. We all are. But not just by our parents or friends or a TV personality. We are wired for connection with our Creator. Yet there's no way we can clean ourselves up enough to make that happen. God doesn't ask us to. Instead He does this: "But God demonstrates his own love for us in this: While we were still sinners, Christ died for us."[3]

For the people in the back, WHILE WE WERE STILL SINNERS, Jesus died for us.

Not after you got your act together or put a shiny filter on your life. Not after you swept all your misdeeds under the rug or tried to compensate for your junk with enough sacrifices and sorries. While you were messy, lonely, ashamed, overwhelmed, broken, and lost, God nailed His love for you to the cross so you could cross the bridge from death to life. Can you imagine a greater kindness?

Scripture says it plainly: "For this is how God loved the world: He gave his one and only Son, so that everyone who believes in him will not perish but have eternal life."[4]

In the words of Paul, "Don't you see how wonderfully kind, tolerant, and patient God is with you? Does this mean nothing to you? Can't you see that his kindness is intended to turn you from your sin?"[5]

If you haven't accepted Christ's payment for all the ways you've missed the mark and fallen short, accepted the free gift of His love and eternal life, you can do that right now.

A gift needs to be received. God's kindness requires a response. The first step is to cross the bridge. Then to show others the way. A life of love and kindness is like arrows pointing people there.

During Jesus's time on earth He shared life with a close group of friends. As He was preparing them to carry on the ministry after His impending death (which His friends didn't fully grasp), Jesus didn't hand over a huge parchment manual with eighty-seven steps on "How to Change the World." He didn't quiz His disciples on the Jewish law. He didn't make them take an oath of perfection or promise to wear a What Would Jesus Do bracelet. Instead He gave them one key instruction:

"A new command I give you: Love one another. As I have loved you, so you must love one another. By this everyone will know that you are my disciples, if you love one another."[6]

*As I have loved you* . . . The heart of the simple difference stems from understanding God's heart toward us. He loves us. Deeply, lavishly, practically, sacrificially. Begin to grasp the love of God, begin to understand how it can transform your life, and you can begin to live a life of transformative kindness. "We love because he first loved us."[7]

I'm so grateful I don't have to carry the burden of perfectly remembering and following a bunch of rules and regulations in order to guarantee my salvation and leave a mark on this world. I'm so grateful Jesus made another way: love God and love others.

As we'll unpack more in the pages to follow, Jesus's expressions of kindness took many different forms. Kindness isn't always conventional. Kindness isn't always tame. It's not wrapped with a bow. Jesus displays a type of kindness that catches people by surprise, gets up in their business, up under their skin. His kindness *is* skin to skin. The kind that washes filthy feet and draws in the dirt instead of throwing stones. The kind that puts mud on eyes, and arms around friends, and touches those whom others deem untouchable, unapproachable, unlovable.

As we look at the threads of who God is, His heart toward people, and how Jesus lived it out, all the strands connect back to the beginning: "So God created mankind in his own image, in the image of God he created them; male and female he created them."[8] In His own image: *imago Dei.* God imprinted His likeness on *every person* who has walked or will walk this earth. Every man, woman, and child has intrinsic, God-given value. He didn't assign more worth to one life and less to another. The way Jesus lived, loved, and served showed that He sees every person as *wonderfully made.* No one is disqualified because of age, ethnicity, job, shady past, or circumstance.

When others condemned, Jesus forgave. When others turned away, Jesus drew near. When others judged and scoffed and made clubs for the haves and have-nots, the good and not-good-enough, Jesus threw His arms wide open and said, "Come." He said let's eat together and sit together. He told them His story and listened to theirs. He didn't reserve His kindness for those who deserved it. Deserving kindness is a myth! None of us deserve it or earn it. The kindness of God is coiled around His mercy and grace—unmerited favor freely given.

Unmerited favor freely given. Wrap your mind around that. Let it wrap around your heart. This is what God extends to us so that we can extend it to others.

The way Jesus saw people made all the difference.

In the same way, *seeing others* as purposeful, beautiful, valuable image bearers of God is foundational to living the simple difference.

Our eyes naturally try to size up how someone looks or acts and then we assign our own meaning to what we observe, which then moves us to respond according to what we think someone deserves. We need some vision retraining. We need to understand, accept, and purpose to see the imago Dei in others. Look for, remember, call out, and honor the divine image in every human vessel.

Do you see how essential this is?

If we merely see people through their actions and outward appearance, we're bound to withhold our love and kindness. When I look around me, I often see people who are irritating, annoying, or off-putting. I see people whose attitudes need adjustments and outlooks need an overhaul. When I see people like this, I don't want to be kind, I want to give them a swift kick in the tush and tell them to get it together! (Yikes, honesty isn't always pretty.)

But when I take off the lens of my own biases and self-interest and put on the lens that shows that every person who irks or offends me is also made in God's image—game changer. My heart begins to soften. Compassion begins to grow. And I remember again that I too am a sinful, irritating person who is loved by God and saved by His grace. I am imago Dei. So are you.

• • •

It should be crystal clear by now that what I propose in this book is not my natural disposition. Please don't think this stuff comes easy for me. I'm no kindness poster child. I'd much rather slap Mister Rogers or Mother Teresa on any billboard to represent the simple difference. My likeness is quick to reveal my gross lack of qualifications.

Kindness is all about love, service, and compassion. Me? Take a gander at the qualities on my kindness résumé:

- impatient
- easily irritable
- self-focused
- introverted
- lover of routines and predictability
- concerned with my own comfort

I hope you're appreciating my intense effort at honest self-reflection and disclosure. I'm doing it so that if you ever get discouraged or feel like you don't have the right personality or temperament for a life marked by kindness, you can come on back here to my little list and know that you're not alone.

Just last night my lack of natural kindness was on display.

My oldest son, Noah, had basketball practice at a time slot that ends later than his normal bedtime, which I find annoying. Then practice inevitably ran long. When it was finally over, we speedwalked down the long ramp from the gymnasium to the car. The cold night air nipped at the quarter inch of ankle exposed between my cuffed jeans and low boots. A chill shot up my whole body. We got in the car and I blasted the heater as Noah chatted about practice. What time was his upcoming game and did I see his layup? I backed out of my parking spot, ready to whip out of the lot and get home, stat. But I couldn't. The coach was standing in the middle of the aisle talking to another parent. I slowly scooted forward, expecting my bright headlights and humming engine would be clear indicators that a motor vehicle would like to drive through the driving area. Please and thank you. The coach took one *small* step to the side. He was still blocking the way.

In this ordinary, Tuesday-night moment, I wasn't thinking about kindness. I was thinking about me. I glared through the dark windshield, willing the coach to see my dagger eyes, have a little consideration, and MOVE out of the way. He didn't. I maneuvered my car as close as I could to the row of parked cars and barely squeezed by.

"Seriously?" I seethed through gritted teeth.

I made a sharp left out of the parking lot, irritated and exasperated that my journey home was delayed by a whopping five minutes. (Okay, it was probably more like ninety seconds . . . or less.) Noah was already inquiring about what was for breakfast tomorrow while flipping through radio stations to find a good song. And like a lyric I couldn't shake, the question rose in my mind, *What happened to the simple difference? What happened to living the big impact of small kindness?*

And here's where I emphasize that I'm not a kindness expert but a broken, jaded, impatient fellow human on the journey—who more often than not feels like a kindness imposter.

I share this because you've got to know this book isn't written by or for the saintly and sinless (which last time I checked is none of us). This book is for you if in the confines of your own car or house or mind you struggle with impatience and irritation, entitlement and apathy. You're welcome here if you make sarcastic comments under your breath. Pull up a chair and lean in if it's easier to think about your own wants, needs, and preferences than someone else's. If you're a good person and you want to do right by the world, but when you're bare-bones honest you have to admit that kindness is *not* your natural inclination either—hi, you're in good company.

I lay in bed last night thinking about how that brief parking lot moment was a missed opportunity to not only show kindness to another human but to model it for my son. I'm sure the coach didn't give it a second thought. My boy probably didn't either. But what if instead of being consumed by my irritation and impatience, I had taken a deep breath? What if I had viewed that extra moment as a gift? To look my son in the eyes. Ask him a question. Listen to the answer.

What if instead of glaring through the windshield I rolled down the window and gave a genuine smile and friendly wave, and offered a sincere, "Thanks again, Coach! I appreciate you investing your time in our boys. Have a great night!" How might that have changed my mood? How might it have touched the man who just gave over an hour of his time to help a scraggly group of eleven-year-olds learn a little more about basketball?

What if instead of living a message of "seriously, hurry up" in front of my son, I let my life speak of slowing down, paying attention, and valuing each person?

Seeing people as individuals whom God loves instead of obstacles to our own comfort and convenience requires us to intentionally change our agenda and perspective.

Here's to slowing down.

Opening our eyes.

Giving our lives.

Remembering that we can love others in backyards, coffee shops, airports, and parking lots—because God first loved us.

## THREE KEYS TO LIVING
*the simple difference*

**Pray it bold.**

*God, thank You for loving me enough to make me in Your image and rescue me from my sin. Help me to grasp the depth of Your loving-kindness so that I can love others in the same way. I want to know Your love as more than a fact in my head but a living knowledge in my heart. Train my vision to see the beauty and value You've handcrafted in every person. Amen.*

**Live it now.**

- Start the day looking in the mirror and reminding yourself that you are loved and chosen by God.
- Consciously practice slowing down in your daily going.
- Notice the people around you and actively remember that they are also loved by God.

**Say it loud.**

I don't have to be a kindness poster child to be a simple difference maker.

*two*

# embrace the awkward

Kindness is a good thing. I can't imagine you or any other dear reader arguing with me on that. We established in the last chapter that we ought to love others because God first loved us. But I'll be the first to raise my hand and admit that the way I treat or respond to people is often not characterized by love and kindness—as my irrationally irritated parking lot incident proves. And I know I'm not alone.

So the question now is: *Why* are we not kind?

I would really rather acknowledge what is working before turning the magnifying glass on the problems. But in this case, I believe we first have to honestly identify the barriers that keep us from choosing kindness before we can move on to the happy hows of living out the simple difference.

If we don't recognize and admit the things that stand in the way of living kindness, we're likely to nod along, as good people tend to do, but in the end remain unchanged.

I'm after change.

Transformation takes more than nice words and agreeing on general principles. Transformation means putting principles into action over and over until new rhythms rewire our hearts and minds. Transformation means not simply tacking on good habits to our existing lives but doing the harder work of untangling ourselves from wrapped-up and warped ideologies or perhaps just harmful complacency.

There's no point in you reading this book (or me writing it) if at the end of it our lives still look the same.

So take a deep breath, friend. This might get bumpy before it gets better. But sometimes you've got to wrestle through the weeds before you can enjoy the outgrowth of freshly tilled soil.

● ● ●

Four of the most common and intertwined barriers that stand in the way of our willingness to show kindness to others are awkwardness, inconvenience, lack of compassion, and snap judgments. Yowza. That's quite the list. If that zings your heart a bit, you're not alone. These tendencies seem innate to human nature, or at the very least ingrained in Western culture.

Most people want to avoid uncomfortable or costly social interaction like the plague. Consider these prescriptions for awkwardness evasion that many of us live by:

- Don't make eye contact with the homeless man or the child with special needs.
- Help a stranger, but only if it doesn't derail your tight schedule or get too complicated—probably better just to mind your own business.
- That person could use a hand up, handout, open door, or second chance—you could give it . . . but doesn't everyone need

38

something? Perhaps their situation is a consequence of their own making.

Have thoughts like these ever crossed your mind? Decide now to answer honestly. Not to me, but to yourself. To get the most out of this simple difference journey, you've got to examine your heart and life openly.

Right beside awkwardness is our aversion to inconvenience. I've walked past a mom in the grocery store parking lot struggling to wrangle her kids while putting groceries in her trunk and thought, *I could help by returning her shopping cart,* but then thought of my own melting ice cream and my desire to squeeze in a few more minutes of work before school pickup, so I didn't offer. A missed opportunity to make a simple difference.

I heard a story nearly a decade ago that I've never been able to shake; it illustrates our fear of awkwardness and inconvenience perfectly. This simple difference moment also takes place in an airport. But I'm not one of the characters. Rather, it's about a famous Bible teacher and a very old man in a wheelchair.

Beth Moore sat in a crowded airport terminal when all heads suddenly snapped in the same direction. Onlooking eyes grew wide and mouths gawked open. Everyone stared behind Beth. She was desperate to see what captured the crowd's attention. Before long, the object of everyone's scrutiny came into her peripheral view.

"It was the oddest sight," she confessed.

In a terminal packed with passengers, there was one open space— right next to Beth. It's there that an airport hostess parked a wheelchair carrying an extremely old man. He was hunched over, nearly folded in half.

As discreetly as she could, Beth glanced over and took in the whole picture. The man's hair was matted and tangled. Long, stringy pieces hung over his downturned face. His nails were as long as any lady's, his pants were oversized and all bunched up. He looked to be about 129 years old, Beth guessed.

The animated Bible teacher went on to share the inner dialogue that ensued when she began to feel the Holy Spirit stir within her. She pleaded with God not to make her witness to this man. "Oh, please, God, no!" she cried inside.

God's reply left Beth slack-jawed: "I'm not asking you to witness to him. I'm asking you to brush his hair."

Can you even imagine?

She then pray-spewed all the reasons she would *love* to witness to him. *What good is combed hair if a man is lost? I am your witness!*

She gave all the reasons brushing a grown man's hair—when she didn't even have a hairbrush—was God's worst idea, pretty much ever.

But Beth knew better than to argue with God for very long. Eventually she surrendered to His leading and mustered up the courage to address the man. She crouched in front of him and meekly said, "Sir, may I have the honor of brushing your hair?"

Of course the ancient stranger was hard of hearing and her soft-spoken request had to be repeated again, and *again*, and AGAIN until the whole terminal whipped their heads around in disbelief as once more she shouted, "Sir, may I have the honor of brushing your hair?!"

Unsure, he replied, "If you want to."

What happened next was the most awkward, beautiful thing. Beth didn't have a hairbrush, but the man said there was one in his bag. She riffled through his undershirts and personal items to find an antique bristle brush. And she brushed his hair. Every matted nest and tangled strand she gently touched. The man explained that he'd been in the hospital for a long time and was finally going home to see his wife.

"I was just sitting here thinking what a mess I must be for my bride."

Who knew how long he had been neglected. Overlooked.

Everyone around Beth kept staring—probably in curiosity, maybe confusion, judgment, or disgust? But now Beth saw only the man. She was consumed with love for him. She was oblivious to everything else around her. Dirty airport carpet had become holy ground and she didn't want to kneel any other place. Beth brushed every strand of hair until it was smooth as silk.

Then she leaned over and asked her new friend, "Do you know Jesus?"

"Yes, I do," he said.

Of course he did.

Eventually it was time for the man to board his plane. Off he went, ready to be reunited with his beloved bride. After a few minutes, the hostess who was escorting him came back out to the terminal. She was crying. Hard.

"What made you do that?" she asked Beth.

"Jesus. He's the bossiest thing."

And then the person who needed to hear the gospel got to hear it.

As Beth told this story to a roomful of women, she summed up the lesson we all see: "[God] knows what our need is! The man didn't need witnessing, he needed his hair brushed."

The airport hostess needed to meet Jesus, but the gentleman who drew every stare? He needed to know he was truly seen, worthy of being cared for. He needed to be shown a little love, dignity, and honor. "When we are filled to the measure with the fullness of Christ," Beth went on, "you cannot believe the needs we can meet. We can do what we know we can't! *That ain't me!* No, it's God."[1]

THIS, my friend, is the heartbeat of the simple difference.

God's Spirit is more powerful than our awkwardness. He can flood us with love that is more real and compelling than our own discomfort or fear of onlookers' opinions. Societal norms and expectations have got nothing on the power of Jesus!

I don't know about you, but I wouldn't want to relive Beth's jaw-dropping story of awkward glory—yet I kinda would. More than guarding my own comfort or reputation, more than protecting myself from awkwardness or inconvenience—I want to live in a way that makes me say without hesitation, *That's not me! I can't do that or say that or love like that. But God can. He's the bossiest thing.*

Are you living in such a way that you're ready to be bossed around by Jesus?

There's no doubt in my mind that there are times the Spirit has stirred my heart . . . and I've ignored Him. No doubt there have been times God has put someone in my path, asked me to say or do something that was just too far outside the cushy boundaries of my comfort zone. No doubt I let my fear of awkwardness rob me (and others) of the impact of obedience, the impact of making a simple difference.

Now, you might argue that what Beth Moore did was not so simple. Brushing an elderly stranger's unkempt hair probably falls in the radical or weird column in most of our books. *Plus, she's a ministry professional*, you might contend. *I'm not that bold or brave. I'm not experienced or trained to serve others in that way.*

To which I'd say, *Yeah. So what?*

If you think about it, while Beth's airport kindness may seem out of the box or over the top, in reality it was quite uncomplicated. It didn't cost her extra time or any money. She didn't seek out the opportunity or go out of her way to be kind. Rather, as she was on her way (or waiting to go on her way, as was the case), she let God have His way with her.

This is what the simple difference is all about. Living with a posture and prayer that says, *Lord, as I go on my way, have Your way with me.*

*Help me to live eyes wide open to the people around me. Empower me*
*to be the blessing in someone's day.*

If you believe you're disqualified from showing love or kindness in
a particular way, you will be. If you think something is possible and
commendable for others, but too awkward or hard or complicated for
you, you've already discounted yourself. Intentional kindness doesn't
require a college degree or certain training or a specific skill set. It
simply requires living with a soft heart surrendered to Jesus.

In speaking about her famous airport incident, Beth said something
I never want to forget: "You have no idea how dangerous you would
be if you would live filled to the measure with the fullness of Christ."[2]
Read that again. "You have no idea how dangerous you would be if you
would live filled to the measure with the fullness of Christ."

I believe in my bones she is right. I want to be that kind of dangerous. I want *you* to be that kind of dangerous.

Imagine if we all were filled to the measure. Imagine if we stopped
playing it safe and got a little awkwardly dangerous for Jesus's name. I
don't know about you, but I want to be compelled out of my comfort zone
for the sake of any man, woman, child, or airport hostess who needs the
love of Christ in the form of hair-brushing or gospel-sharing or whatever
other ordinary, radical thing that might meet the need in front of me.

It's time to let Jesus up in our business and boss us around a bit.

• • •

Jesus was known for getting up in people's business during His time
on earth. He liked to flip tables. Overturn twisted and outdated prac-
tices. Turn societal expectations upside down and inside out.

He did this one day when a religious leader and expert of the law,
sometimes called a lawyer, tried to test Jesus by asking what he must
do to inherit eternal life.

Jesus replied with a question of His own. "What is written in the Law? How do you read it?" The lawyer replied: "Love the Lord your God with all your heart and with all your soul and with all your strength and with all your mind," and "Love your neighbor as yourself."

He was quoting Scripture from modern-day Deuteronomy 6:5 and Leviticus 19:18. Jesus affirmed his answer and told him to do these things and he would live.

But the religious leader wasn't satisfied. He wanted to justify his actions and beliefs—to defend his own righteousness—so he asked, "And who is my neighbor?"

In other words, the guy was looking for a loophole.

It's this question that launches Jesus into a story that shocked His original audience and should shake us up good too. The whole scene plays out in Luke 10:25–37 in what has become known as the parable of the Good Samaritan. Here's the quick recap: There is a man robbed, beaten, stripped, and left for dead on the road to Jericho. A priest and a Levite pass by, one at a time, see the dying man, and cross to the other side. Then a Samaritan comes along and has compassion on the battered stranger. The Samaritan bandages his wounds, carries him on his donkey into the next village, cares for him overnight at an inn, then pays the innkeeper to continue to nurse the man back to health.

Jesus concludes by pointing back to the religious leader's precipitating question: "Which of these three do you think was a neighbor to the man who fell into the hands of robbers?" The expert in the law answers that it was the one who showed mercy. Jesus's response is simple, "Go and do likewise."

Okay, talk about awkwardness and inconvenience. There is so much for us to learn and unpack in this story.

The first thing that would have stood out to the original listeners would have been the stark contrast in religious and racial differences between the first two Jewish men who traveled the road and the Samaritan who came after them. The former were high-ranking temple leaders, the latter a foreigner despised by Jews. The Samaritan would have been the natural villain to a Jewish audience, so the fact that he is the one who comes out as the shining example at the end would have been shocking to the crowd listening to Jesus tell this story.

But beyond their outward distinctions, there are two primary characteristics that make the Samaritan in the story stand out from the priest and the Levite: compassion and a correctly applied definition of being a neighbor.

"Neighbor" is the Greek word *plesion*, which is a general term for neighbor "expressing the idea of one's fellow human being."[3] But as one commentary explains, "The lawyer's question is really an attempt to create a distinction, arguing that some people are neighbors and others are not, and that one's responsibility is only to love God's people. The suggestion that some people are 'non-neighbors' is what Jesus responds to in his story."[4]

From my present-day perspective, I'm quick to wag my mental finger at the teacher of the law and his seemingly self-serving query.

*Who is my neighbor?*

*Dude, everyone's your neighbor!* I want to shout back.

Today we know that God loves *all* people, which is why Jesus died for *all*. (If you still don't believe this, go back and read the last chapter.) But before Christ, there was no "all." There were God's people—the Jews—and everybody else—the gentiles. Neighbor and non-neighbor. Jesus changed that. He demonstrated throughout His life and ministry, and ultimately His death and resurrection, that relationships trump religiosity.

Eternal life is not about upholding laws but loving people.

Compassion supersedes following regulations.

Both in service to the Jewish temple, the priest and Levite were under strict obligation to closely follow rules for physical cleanliness. Touching a man covered in his own blood and body fluids definitely would have fallen into the *not clean* category. The people listening to the parable would have known this. *Jesus* would have known this! But again, Jesus takes what is known off the pedestal of perceived priority and shows people what really matters—people.

The priest and the Levite both had the religious training to know the commands to love God and love their neighbors, but they were living the wrong definition of neighbor. The Samaritan, on the other hand, was not a Jew, not a man learned in Scripture, but he was the better and surprising example of what being a neighbor means. "But a Samaritan, as he traveled, came where the man was; and when he saw him, he took pity on him."[5]

The one who acted as a neighbor was the one who showed compassion.

Call me a nerd, but this gets my brain spinning and synapses firing. The connection is unmistakable. Do you see how perfectly this story illustrates what it means to live the simple difference? As he traveled— going wherever he was going—the Samaritan saw a person in need. He was on his way, but he was aware of those around him. He noticed. And he chose to respond with kindness. Mr. Samaritan Man could basically be our Simple Difference Parable Poster Child.

Okay, there's more. Hang with me. Jesus said the Samaritan took pity on the beaten man. Pity in this sense is "a tender, considerate feeling for others, ranging from judicial clemency through kindness and mercy to compassion."[6] The Greek word for pity, *splanchnizomai*, can also be translated as compassion. But unlike this first definition suggests, compassion is not only a feeling someone has; it's an action they do. *Splanchnizomai* is a verb—to be moved with compassion.[7]

Do you see the dots connecting back to our earlier story about Beth Moore? Beth was *splanchnizomai* for the man in the airport wheelchair. She didn't simply feel bad for his scraggly hair and off-putting appearance. She was moved by compassion (and the Spirit's leading) to help him.

Likewise, the Samaritan did not simply *feel* sorry for the beaten man. He didn't just think, *Oh, that's a shame,* or *Bad break for that guy,* or even *I hope he doesn't suffer too long.* No, his compassion moved him to action. "He went to him and bandaged his wounds, pouring on oil and wine. Then he put the man on his own donkey, brought him to an inn and took care of him. The next day he took out two denarii and gave them to the innkeeper. 'Look after him,' he said, 'and when I return, I will reimburse you for any extra expense you may have.'"[8]

Do you think this was part of the Samaritan's plan for his day? Of course not! No doubt it was a total inconvenience. It cost him time and money. It likely had implications for his job and family. And yet every time I read this story, I see ever more clearly that the Samaritan loved the way he would want someone to love him. If you or I were robbed of our possessions and the clothes off our backs, if we were stranded on the side of a busy freeway or country road, broken down, beaten up, and taken advantage of, would we not want someone to stop what they were doing and show us compassion?

*Please, Jesus, send someone to help!* we would cry.

The command to "Love your neighbor as yourself" is God's way of responding in advance to those cries. The question is, will we choose to *be* the blessing, *be* the help, *be* the answer to someone's prayer? I hope so. I want to be.

The feeling side of compassion is often where we get stuck. At least that's true for me. I see someone in trouble, someone hurting or helpless, and I honestly feel sorry for their sorrow. I wish their hard circumstances were different.

But how am I being a neighbor by just wishing their predicament was fixed? I'm not.

People also get stuck the same way that the priest and the Levite did, by living with the wrong definition of neighbor. Few of us consciously think this or would be willing to admit it. "Of course loving my neighbor means loving everyone," we'd be quick to say. But too often our biases and judgments, aided by the queen of our own comfort and convenience, rule our decision-making in such a way that we do *not*, in fact, live like everyone is our neighbor. Each of us must search our own heart (and ask God to help us!) to identify and confess our prejudice. Maybe we think someone isn't our neighbor—isn't worthy of our help—if they make too much money, or not enough. Maybe our working definition of neighbor means people who dress like us or speak the same language as us. Maybe we think neighbor means people who are warm and friendly, people who wave hello and take in their trash cans on time.

But let's not forget how Jesus posed his closing question in the parable: "Which of these three do you think was a neighbor to the man who fell into the hands of robbers?" Loving our neighbor starts with *being* a neighbor.

It's not how we classify others but how we choose to love. Realizing we all belong to each other because we all belong to God.

The expert of the law answered Jesus's question: "The one who had mercy on him."

Jesus told him, "Go and do likewise."[9]

*Go and do likewise.* May we each take this as our charge to change the world by being a neighbor who shows mercy and compassion to others.

• • •

Many years ago I witnessed my husband have his own Good Samaritan moment, and I'll never forget it. It wasn't quite as dramatic as helping a naked, bloodied man left for dead. But he did step in when others overlooked and passed by a neighbor in need.

We found ourselves in the emergency room with our eight-month-old, trying to figure out the cause of his twelve-day-long fever. The ER was exceptionally crowded. Patients and concerned family members filled up the waiting room and spilled outside. The air was thick with heat and humidity, more than normal for a spring evening. Adults groaned in pain. Children fussed. Everyone coughed. It was going to be a long night. And more disheartening (and hopeful) than I imagined.

An hour into our wait in the dingy, disease-infested waiting room, a hospital orderly passed a few feet in front of a woman wheezing for breath. She waved her hand to solicit his help. He turned and looked right at her—but kept on walking. Chris and I both did a double take. *Did he really just blatantly ignore her?* The worker exited the front door. He returned with a wheelchair for another patient.

The next thing I knew, my husband was gone from the seat next to me and was standing in front of the worker. "Excuse me, why didn't you stop and help that woman?" Chris asked. "You saw her waving her hand, pleading for help, but you walked right by without even acknowledging her. Why?"

"It's not my job," the man responded.

Chris went on to explain that helping people *is*, in fact, his job.

Meanwhile as this exchange was happening, the woman was still gesturing for help. There was a whole crew of hospital staff members huddled behind the reception desk, gawking at the scene.

"Is anyone going to help her?" Chris asked. "It seems like she needs some water."

"She can't have any water," was the receptionist's dry reply.

At that moment, the distressed patient finally found her voice and yelled out that she needed a vomit bag.

Again, no one moved. The entire waiting room stared silent and stiff, save for a few stifled coughs. My blood pressure rose at the lack of compassion being shown by everyone but my husband.

"Is anybody going to help her?!" Chris exclaimed.

"Yes, sir, we have it taken care of," shot a cool voice with an icy look from behind the counter.

Eventually the woman was given a paper bag to puke in. But her dignity was already lost.

Later in the night, when we were still waiting, a staff member emerged from the treatment area. *Please let it be our turn,* I prayed as I felt my baby's burning forehead again. Instead she called another name. A small, elderly woman stood and began to gather half a dozen grocery bags piled at her feet. The staffer passed the patient and said, "Follow me."

The hospital worker saw the large load the patient was trying to carry but didn't offer to help. In fact, she didn't even pause. She sized up the situation and then continued her brisk pace. (Sound like a certain priest or Levite?)

Again, Chris and I exchanged a look of dismay.

Earlier we had overheard the EMT who assisted this patient inside relay to the check-in staff that the woman had been in a car accident and had a large laceration on her head—information that would have been clearly stated on the patient's chart.

This time Chris didn't say a word.

He just got up and rushed to the shaken woman's side. He gently took the grocery sacks out of her frail hands. Together they tried to catch up with the worker but trailed the whole way down a series of long hospital halls. The injured patient thanked my husband more than a dozen times. The hospital employee said nothing.

Now, I realize this one evening is not representative of all hospital workers. Healthcare professionals—from those performing surgery to those sanitizing toilets—are some of the most remarkable and self-sacrificing people on earth! Yet, similar to the priest and Levite who were also in the "business" of serving people, the ER staff that night demonstrated how easy it is for people to become so callous to their jobs that they lose common courtesy, decency, and respect for their fellow humans. Compassion was painfully absent.

As sick to my stomach as those incidents made me, my heart burst with love and appreciation for the courteous, decent, and respectful man I married. Chris wasn't trying to be a hero. He was just doing the right thing. The kind thing.

He was willing to see the people around him and let compassion move him to take action. One word, one helping hand at a time.

Kindness means speaking up, stepping in, showing love even (or especially) when others choose not to. If you ever feel queasy over the injustice in this world. If your blood boils over how people are overlooked, mistreated, or just made the object of a crowd's fascination, *you* can be the one to make a difference.

Be bold. Be awkward. Be inconvenienced.

It's not always easy, but it is pretty simple. Let compassion move you. This is how we make our mark.

**Pray it bold.**

*Jesus, thank You for valuing relationships over religious perfor-mance. I give You access to my comfort and my biases. Replace them with Your compassion. Empower me today to embrace the next hard, awkward, or inconvenient opportunity to love a neigh-bor. Amen.*

**Live it now.**

- Lean into the gift of awkwardness today by showing kindness in a way that's outside your comfort zone.
- When an inconvenient opportunity to help comes your way, think about how you would want to be loved.
- If someone is being mistreated, step in and speak up. Do what you can to help that person know they matter.

**Say it loud.**

Jesus, get bossy with me.

*three*

# every word counts

In the early days of motherhood, worn-out running shoes and a rickety double stroller were the threadbare tie to my sanity. Daily I tied up those laces like I was girding my flailing ability to mother. I strapped the three-year-old in the front stroller seat, the two-year-old in the rear, and doled out an abundance of snacks and sippy cups. I prayed their wiggly bodies would calm under the three-point-harness security. If not, at least they were contained.

I hoisted the baby into the strappy apparatus attached to my chest. Tiny sun hat and pacifier, check. Burp cloth tucked in my back pocket in case the morning's projectile spit-up wasn't quite finished, check. We were ready to go. Me and my boys.

My feet pounded the pavement as I strained to propel my precious cargo forward. I pushed harder, trying to relieve the pressure that pressed from the inside. I was out of breath before I made it to the end of the block. The boys babbled to one another about kitties perched in picture windows and earthworms squished flat on driveways.

I battled my thoughts.

*Just go home! You're sleep-deprived and out of shape. Why torture yourself this way? Turn on the TV for them and go back to bed.*

But then I'd hear, *No, you need this. Stay the course. You'll find your rhythm. It will get easier. Just breathe. Just breathe.*

As much as my legs hurt and lungs burned, I had to keep going. Fresh air and moving your body—no matter how squishy it is—gets the endorphins flowing. The combination is like soul medicine. I needed a strong dose.

I turned toward the foothills aglow with morning light and made my way to the quaint main street just coming alive. Shop owners turned on lights, hot coffeepots steamed as servers in maroon aprons filled mugs for customers huddled around small sidewalk tables.

The wobbly left stroller wheel clunked hard over another concrete bulge. The baby kicked his legs and his tiny sock fell off. I paused to pick it up, sip some water, kiss each toddler.

I kept pushing north until the shops fell behind us. Historic bungalows and craftsman homes now lined the wide street. Ample sidewalks flanked each side. A tree overloaded with bright yellow blossoms popped gloriously against the blue sky.

My toddlers both started to squirm under their buckles, fussing that they needed more snacks. Noah dragged his foot against the sidewalk. Elias leaned over the edge of the stroller, stretching his chubby fingers toward a nearby rosebush. He shrieked when it was out of reach. I turned at the top of the long street to make our descent. My back was aching, and Jude was stirring from his short snooze.

"No, Mommy doesn't have any more Goldfish, and your buns need to sit down right now!"

By the time we walked back down the street, I'd stopped a dozen times to discipline, soothe, or redirect a child. I *may* have breathed through gritted teeth a bribe involving sitting nicely without whining and getting to watch *Curious George* when we got home or threatened an unpleasant alternative.

As the sun rose higher in the sky, the Village shops and stores were bustling with more people, which somehow made me feel both comforted and more alone.

I looked ahead and saw customers filling the outdoor seating area of another little breakfast diner. A group of older men crowded around two tables pushed together. Their chairs spilled over into the sidewalk. It would be tight to squeeze by.

"Keep your arms and legs inside the stroller," I reminded the boys as we approached. I was sweating.

Just then one of the gentlemen stood up. I thought he was going to scoot his chair out of the way to give me more room to pass by, but instead he started clapping. Then he declared in a deep booming voice, "Here comes Super Mom! Make way for Super Mom! Let's give her a hand!" And together, as if on cue, his retired comrades all joined in a spontaneous standing ovation for me and my little crew.

"A round of applause for Super Mom!" he cheered.

I was so caught off guard all I could do was offer a bewildered smile and keep on walking. But it didn't take too many paces before my vision blurred with tears.

This unexpected kindness struck me to my core.

I was walking downhill, but it was hard to catch my breath.

What could have prompted such a spontaneous act of encouragement? This grandfatherly man might have been impressed to see a mom with three tiny kids out and about so early in the morning. Perhaps I looked like a motherhood pro with my three brown-eyed sons lined up in a row. Maybe he had a daughter in my same life stage and knew how much moms need encouragement. Or he could have been just a jolly soul who liked stirring up attention and making people smile. Whatever the reason for his sidewalk outburst of applause, there's no way Mr. Kind Stranger could have known that beneath my sunglasses and smile was a mom barely hanging on.

Tears eventually slid down my cheeks as I turned onto our street. But they didn't fall on the strained grimace I wore at the start of the walk. No, I let that Super Mom smile stay stretched across my face, catching every salty drop of gratitude.

Simple words of encouragement are the uncomplicated gift we can give without cost or limit. A genuine compliment, a heartfelt thank-you, a sincere apology. There are a million ways to tell a neighbor or stranger that you see her, that she is not forgotten. *You are valuable. Your pain matters. You're doing a great job. You inspire me.*

Do not underestimate the power of kind words.

I thought about that Super Mom comment for weeks. As I took my kids to the pediatrician, as I struggled to find another way to cook chicken, as I buckled under the weight of taking care of three littles while working from home at a job that was not my joy but helped pay the bills, in the rare quiet moments before I drifted off to sleep, the refrain of encouragement quietly rose in my heart. "A round of applause for Super Mom!"

Each time I recalled those words, I took a deep breath and knew that I could keep on keeping on.

• • •

Sometimes we try to make making a difference complicated. We think it takes a lot of time or special skills or more money than we have to give.

The doubts come tumbling out.

*How can a regular person like me really change the trajectory of society? Surely the weight of the world's problems can't be easily lifted.*

*People's pain can't be magically erased. The pieces of our individual and collective brokenness can't just be picked up and glued back together like a porcelain plate. Complex issues don't have simple solutions. So if I'm not someone in a position of great power or grand influence, how can I really be part of big-scale change that matters? I can't cure cancer or end racism by clapping for a stranger. It's not like I'm actually going to help the world's hunger problem by simply being nice or making my kids eat their vegetables.*

I'm voicing the honest thoughts and questions I find myself grappling with. Maybe your doubts, concerns, or excuses take on a different tone. Whatever they are, it's important to call them out.

Be it misconceptions, fears, or excuses rooted in our own comfort, we've got to keep identifying and naming the things that hold us back from being agents of change.

For starters, one of mine—and maybe it's yours too—is the false belief that kindness is synonymous with niceness. We think of a person who is kind as someone who acts politely, gives generously, and doesn't rock the boat.

But Jesus rocked the boat.

Jesus was the ultimate example of kindness, yet somehow He still flipped tables in the temple courts when money changers made a mockery of His Father's house. Jesus was kind, but he didn't hold back from calling people out for their favoritism, legalism, and hypocrisy. Kind doesn't mean being a pushover. Kindness is brave. While simple, kindness can also be bold and risky and often costly to self. That's pretty much the Jesus way.

Secondly, let's remind ourselves that individual lives are no less important than big-scale change. We can do for one what we wish we could do for all. Sure, I may not be able to end world hunger, resolve homelessness, or eradicate mental illness. But can I provide a meal for one person? Will a full belly mean something to that someone? Yes. Yes, it will.

Living the simple difference is recognizing that we can't always be problem solvers, but we can be people see-ers. Go ahead and read that again. We can't always be problem solvers, but we can be people see-ers. And this is perhaps one of the most radical and life-changing ways we can wield our words.

I've learned the power of seeing people, especially in their pain, from my friend Michele Cushatt, a three-time cancer survivor and someone well acquainted with hardship and trauma of many kinds. Michele shared a story several years ago that stuck to my soul. Read it in her own words:

I reached to shake his hand. Instead, he shrank back and pulled away. Confused, I looked at his face and then his hand. That's when I saw the bandages.

"Burns," he told me. While attending the funeral of a relative and caring for the needs of the extended family, a pot of boiling oil on the stove had exploded, splattering his face and chest as well as the hand that held the handle.

"It's been two weeks," he said. "It's much better now. You should have seen it when it happened."

From my angle, his wounds still looked painful and raw. I could see the darkening red blisters and blackened scabs covering face, neck, arms. But the most severe burns were covered by bandages on his hand and nose. I could only imagine the pain this man endured.

He'd heard me speak earlier that day, knew about my own burns and scars. In a room of over a thousand church and ministry leaders, I'd shared my undone story through years of extreme head and neck cancer and treatment, and the wrestling and refining of my faith in the process. Although the source of our suffering was different, the shared experience of it connected us. We understood each other, fellow members of this same hard family of pain.

"People say stupid things." He smiled. But the smile didn't quite reach his eyes. "Like the ones who tell me 'It could've been so much worse' and 'Why didn't you . . . ?' and 'You're lucky!' They think they're helping, but they're not."

Though well-meaning, these people and their comments add to the pain, I knew. Even this week yet one more person offered to send me a detailed letter of how I could cure myself, the foods and supplements and treatments and oils I should use to alleviate my suffering. As if I haven't already tried everything.

As if my pain is my fault.

But not all are as misdirected. My new friend and I then talked about the sweet gift of those rare souls who, rather than trying to cure our pain or deflect it, step into it with us.

Rather than blame, they *bear*.

That's when he looked me in the eye and said with an empathy I knew was hard-earned:

"I'm so sorry for your suffering."

I let the words land, allowing them to soak and soften the brittle places. Then, I smiled. Nodded. And offered the very same words back to him.

And we both agreed, to the person in a place of pain, that's all that is needed.

———

*I'm so sorry for your suffering.*

Those six words envelope the kindness of acknowledging someone's pain. I can imagine Jesus saying that to the woman who bled for twelve long years. To the leper and blind man before He healed their plight. *I'm so sorry for your suffering.* Jesus entered into pain. He invites us to do the same.

Michele went on to explain why our response is often less than helpful and how we can learn to love better.

---

The problem is, however, we want to say more, do more. Pain makes us uncomfortable, even if it isn't our own. Maybe especially then. So we try to distance ourselves from it by offering cliches and cures, maxims and memes. But in our effort to make suffering more manageable, we actually neglect those in the middle of it.

What if we started being more intentional with our attempts at empathy? What if we started practicing new words, new offerings, rather than continuing to use the tired old ones?

Rather than filling space with our platitudes, let's make space with our presence.

And rather than offering our unsolicited solutions, let's make space for questions and then listen to the answers.

*What do you need most right now?*

*What's the most difficult part of this for you?*

*How can I love you well right here?*

And *I'm so sorry for your suffering.*

These are the words the person who suffers needs to hear most. Because they communicate nearness, presence, and make the person in pain feel less alone.

To those who were exhausted, beat up, worn down, and overwhelmed, Jesus entered in. He didn't add blame and shame to those already bent over with the weight of their burden. And He didn't deliver a three-point directive of self-cures and solutions.

Instead, He offered all of Himself, for all that we need:

> Come to me, all you who are weary and burdened, and I will give you rest. Take my yoke upon you and learn from me, for I am gentle and humble in heart, and you will find rest for your souls. For my yoke is easy and my burden is light. (Matt. 11:28–30 NIV)

Gentleness. Steadfastness. And Presence in the middle of pain.[1]

The next time you're faced with someone's pain, what will you say? Will you minimize or empathize? Will you try to solve the problem, or will you resolve to just bear witness to their anguish? Most often people don't need a reminder of how much worse their circumstances could be or advice for how to overcome their challenge. They just need someone to come alongside them.

In my pain, I just need someone to acknowledge and be with me. Isn't the same true for you?

Let's use our words to help others know they are seen and not alone.

• • •

Here's another story about the gift of seeing others and saying so.

We accidentally got to the library eight minutes early. On the surface this doesn't seem like a big deal . . . but with three spirited boys, eight extra minutes can feel like eight hours. At the time, my sons were seven, six, and four—the perfect ages for high curiosity and low impulse control. As we entered the small outer foyer and I realized the main library wasn't open yet, low-grade panic set in. My kids were not cut from the "sit still and wait patiently" kind of cloth.

Thankfully we had a bag full of books to return. *Let's draw this out as long as possible*, I thought. Each boy excitedly took turns feeding picture books into the automated return system. They oohed and aahed as the scanner scanned each barcode and the title appeared on the nearby screen (and then they shoved a brother to get a better look) as the conveyor belt carried each book to the appropriate bin. Dump. *Again!*

When our book bag was empty, they slurped water from the drinking fountain, hid under the massive stairwell, asked a gazillion questions about what would happen if the concrete cracked and fell on top of them and would they for sure be crushed and die? There were two trips to the bathroom and a thorough investigation of a row of cupboards that foolishly were void of padlocks. As the minutes inched on, more library patrons joined my energetic crew in the waiting vestibule. Staring eyes weren't in short supply.

"Be aware of others. Stay near me. Quiet words, please," I reminded them often.

My boys weren't being bad. Just inquisitive, antsy, talkative, active kids. And after eight minutes, their mama was exhausted. When the clock struck ten and the bell tower began to chime, the large sliding glass doors finally opened. The small crowd began filing into the sanctuary of books. Jude jumped and Elias squealed and Noah started to sprint as I reminded them *again* to please walk and use inside voices.

An older woman who had been waiting nearby caught my eye. "It's going to be a long summer," she said.

"Yeah, it is," I replied with a weak smile and sigh.

Then her eyes brightened, and her smile warmed. "But you're doing a great job. Thank you for being here," she added.

I had braced myself for a stranger's rebuke—parenting in public is one of the hardest things for me. In the little years it made me sweat with anxiety. But instead of judgment I was met with the kindness of simple encouragement. All I could do was whisper *thank you*. She gave me a knowing nod and entered the library as I followed my sons—my back a bit straighter, my steps a bit lighter.

A small, unexpected thank-you from a stranger. A word to make someone feel seen. Is there an easier gift of kindness to give?

So I pass on these sweet words to you: *Thank you.* Thank you for changing diapers and reading stories. Thank you for going to work and still making dinner when you're dog-tired. Thank you for cheering at swim lessons and folding laundry and answering the billionth question to quench a little person's curiosity. Thank you for helping your neighbor and listening to your coworker. Thanks for getting to church early to set up or staying late to tear down. Thanks for mentoring that teenager. Thanks for doing your mundane job with a smile. Thanks for putting one foot in front of the other.

Thank you for being you. No one else could fill your shoes.

• • •

Are you beginning to see what a significant impact a small word of encouragement can make in someone's day? *Green is a great color on you. You love well. I'm impressed by how you handled that.* There are limitless possibilities for how we can build up others.

Proverbs 16:24 explains the significance of our words: "Kind words are like honey—sweet to the soul and healthy for the body" (NLT). I can't count the times that my soul has been revived by the sweetness of someone's words. Kind words have saved me from teetering over the edge of spiritual doubt and physical exhaustion. A timely word of encouragement has reeled me in from emotional overwhelm and mental fatigue. When I've spiraled into the black pit of anxiety and depression, words that remind me that I am loved as I am have made all the difference.

Most often the person speaking these words had no idea how desperately I needed a lifeline woven from the threads of kindness.

Just this week I got a voice message from a friend. She asked how specific areas of my life were going. Asked how she could pray. In addition to making space for me to share my heart—the good and the hard—she also made a point to tell me how much she appreciated something I had recently written on Instagram. She said she could tell I was being intentional with my words and investing in my online community. She didn't know that in that moment I had been feeling discouraged, wondering if my voice on a noisy app really mattered.

She reminded me I mattered. To her. To others. And to God. She told me He was pleased with me.

I saved that message and I've listened to it twice. I'll probably listen to it again. Sometimes we need to hear what we already know.

Sometimes we just need to know we're valued, celebrated, seen. Think back to how a well-timed word of kindness or encouragement has made a difference in your life. Perhaps a coworker complimented you on a job you thought nobody noticed. Maybe a friend told you how much they valued you right when you were feeling overlooked. Or perhaps a barista handed you your latte and paused to say how much he loved your hair. Whether a comment is fleeting or it lingers, encouraging words mark the hearts of both the giver and receiver.

Consider how you can lavish the simple kindness of encouragement on those around you. As you go on your way, here are ten easy things you can say to encourage someone today:

1. I see you.

2. I'm proud of you.

3. God made you beautiful.

4. You shine doing that thing you're created to do.

5. I'm thankful for you.

6. You inspire me.

7. I appreciate your hard work.

8. God delights in you.

9. You make my day brighter.

10. I'm grateful to call you friend.

Look for that frazzled mom in the grocery store or that shy coworker in the corner cubicle. Think of your best friend or the school secretary, the crossing guard or bus driver you pass every day. Stop and say, "Thank you for being here. You're doing a great job. Your life makes mine better."

My favorite thing about this is that the power of words is available, accessible, wieldable for everyone. No one is disqualified from being an encourager.

Whether you're a college student or a retired teacher. Whether you've got lots of littles hanging all over you or lots of deadlines hanging over your head. If you're chronically ill, underemployed, or climbing the corporate ladder. If you're happily married or happily single or going through a life-breaking divorce. No matter who you are, where you live, or what your circumstances are in this very moment, YOU can make a difference in someone's life just with the simple tools of lips, teeth, and tongue (or moving hands and fingers, for those who communicate in the beautiful language of sign). Regardless of the language you speak, how old you are, how good or hard, stressed or blessed your life feels today, *you* can make an impact.

You can encourage a fellow human to keep on keeping on. One word at a time.

• • •

Certainly the apostle Paul understood the power of caring for people with intentional kindess when he charged believers in Colossae with this command: "Therefore, as God's chosen people, holy and dearly loved, clothe yourselves with compassion, kindness, humility, gentleness and patience."[2]

Every day we get to choose what we're going to put on. To be honest, some days I unconsciously slip into the easy ways of self-focus, just like pulling on yesterday's worn jeans. They're crumpled on the floor, and without even thinking, they're suddenly zipped, buttoned, and covering half my body. When I operate on wardrobe-autopilot for my spirit, the same thing happens. I'm suddenly immersed in my day without recognizing that I'm covered with distraction instead of compassion. I've put on a me-first attitude instead of kindness, pride instead of humility, a harsh spirit instead of gentleness, annoyance rather than patience. It's not a becoming look. But even more than that, these layers shroud my spiritual vision.

When we're wrapped in these kinds of self-focused coverings, we're not able to notice, we're not ready to respond to, the people around us. That's why Paul makes it clear that we must be intentional about what we put on. But take note of this, friend: It's not only important *what* we put on every day but *why*. Before jumping to the desired action, Paul prefaces it with our divine identity: "Therefore, as God's chosen people, holy and dearly loved."[3] We put on love and kindness *because* we are completely loved. We are daughters and sons of God! That's what it means to be chosen. You're not the leftover or last pick or the short straw that got drawn. You were chosen. Keep that truth in your mind as you move through this book.

Knowing who you are is crucial to knowing why you do what you do.

I know I'm a writer, so I write. I'm a mother, so I mother. I'm a beloved, chosen child of God, heir to the King, friend of Jesus, home to the Holy Spirit, so I live like it—by His strength!

I am loved, so I love.

As we've read before, "We love because he first loved us."[4]

You are loved—therefore you are called to love.

Today, let's love with the power of simple encouragement. Let's put on the love and kindness of Jesus. Let's be people who live eyes wide open to the next opportunity to make every word count. To speak up for injustice. To infuse courage into weary parents. To let every person know that their pain and joy and story matters.

Today you have a chance to leave a word-shaped mark on someone's heart. Right where you are.

## THREE KEYS TO LIVING
### *the simple difference*

**Pray it bold.**

*God, I know words are powerful and I want to use mine well. Get rid of my fear and timidity, remove the barriers of my own busyness, distractions, and biases. Show me today who You want to encourage. Make me bold to build others up. Make my words Yours and use them to mark someone's heart with kindness. Amen.*

**Live it now.**

- Call or text a friend: ask them how that hard thing is going, tell them what you value most in them.
- Give a stranger a genuine compliment or word of encouragement; linger long enough to hear their response.
- Start your day with the intentional decision to put on love, kindness, and compassion.

**Say it loud.**

I will mark the world, one kind word at a time.

*four*

# not your last resort

It startled me the first time it happened. It was a Wednesday night my freshman year of college at the musty YMCA behind my dorm. That's where my collegiate ministry met. After our weekly worship and teaching, we milled around afterward in small groups. Scuffing our feet on the thin, dingy carpet, laughing easily, procrastinating going back to whatever late-night studying or paper-writing awaited us.

I was talking with my friend Kathy. We were probably sharing the highs and lows of the week or commiserating over how the dining hall ran out of chicken crispitos at dinner. I don't recall the exact details of our conversation—I'm sure it involved me venting about my latest stress-inducing situation with school or the guy I was dating, not dating, or wanting to date again. But through the fog of more than twenty years, I do remember clearly what happened next.

"Let me pray for you about that," Kathy said.

And then she put her hand on my shoulder and started to pray.

She didn't say, "I will pray for you about that," as in, after we leave or tomorrow before class or later in the week if I happen to remember. She just did it—right there under the buzzing fluorescent lights with our friends cracking jokes nearby and the worship band tearing down their equipment. Kathy prayed.

Telling this story now doesn't seem so radical. My friend prayed for me. So what? But at the time? As an eighteen-year-old feeling fresh and stretched in my faith-growing skin, it was the most unexpected, exhilarating thing. I felt so . . . cared for. Loved. Seen.

Kathy's prayer didn't last long. Standing there with my eyes closed in the middle of a bunch of other college students felt awkward. But as we've already learned, maybe simple words and a healthy dose of awkwardness are the very things that can point another person to Jesus. It did for me.

That wouldn't be the last time a friend showed me the kindness of praying in the moment. Just last week at church, I found my friend Margie during the "meet and greet" time between worship songs. Immediately, her sweet face lit up, and she pulled me into the type of warm hug grandmothers give best. Then she took my hand and asked how my writing was coming and how my kids were doing. I told Margie that the boys were good and I had recently finished a huge project. But I would be getting edits back soon, and I needed God to expand my capacity because I was in the middle of an extra-busy season at work.

There in the middle of a cacophony of chitchat, with friends and strangers shaking hands across rows of chairs, Margie pulled me back in for a hug and prayed. "Lord, increase Becky's time and energy this week. Use her talents for the good of Your kingdom and to encourage the hearts of women. You are so faithful. We know You will do it. Amen."

I inhaled my friend's rose perfume and smiled at the life of faith etched across her face. An extra dose of joy and peace transferred from her to me in our final squeeze. I felt held up.

Margie could have promised to pray for me that week, and I know she would have been true to her word. But to stop and do it right there was kind and bold and a gift to my heart. As the worship leader started strumming his guitar again, I made my way back to my seat, reminded in that moment of what I needed most: to be assured of God's faithfulness. His fierce with-ness.

We often treat prayer like a last resort. Now, I don't know anyone who would admit this in their theology, but the belief is often revealed in our actions. When we know someone is going through something hard—a relationship is broken or finances are stretched, a diagnosis comes or it's just a regular stressful Tuesday—a common sentiment slips easily from our lips that sounds something like this: "I wish there was something I could do to help, but at least I'll pray."

Prayer was never meant for the "at least" column.

When you really want to be there for someone who is in a predicament or show you care in a time of crisis, you can at least make a casserole or bring in the trash cans or pick up milk and toilet paper. At the very least you can write a check or put away the dishes or pick up some Trader Joe's flowers. These small gestures of thoughtfulness might go in the "at least" category of coming alongside a fellow human in their time of need. But not prayer.

Prayer is not a last resort; it's our first response.

We don't pray because there's nothing else we can do. We pray because that's exactly the most powerful thing we can do.

The apostle Paul told Timothy, "I urge, then, *first of all*, that petitions, prayers, intercession and thanksgiving be made for all people."[1] Paul also instructed the believers in Philippi, "Do not be anxious about anything, but in every situation, by prayer and petition, with thanksgiving, present your requests to God."[2] What greater way to make an immediate and lasting impact on someone's life than taking their cares directly to God?

Prayer is not meant to be only our first response, it's also our most powerful simple difference rhythm. We see examples of constant and continual prayer all over Scripture. Certainly Jesus's ministry is marked by prayer. He often stopped to pray with His disciples or went away alone to pray.[3] Jesus even "told his disciples a parable to show them that they should *always pray* and not give up."[4]

Prayer was also a cornerstone of Paul's ministry. Again and again in his letters, he tells his friends and fellow early church members that he is praying for them. He impresses the importance of prayer in his final instructions of his first letter to the Thessalonians: "Rejoice always, pray continually, give thanks in all circumstances; for this is God's will for you in Christ Jesus."[5] Want to do God's will? Pray all the time. What does that mean? Talk to God. Talk to God with people and on behalf of people.

There is no clearer path to making a difference in this world than the one marked by an ongoing dialogue with God.

Kathy was a good friend. As a good friend, she could have given me advice about my guy problem or offered to help me study for my upcoming exam. Margie could have brought over dinner or offered to babysit my kids to free up some time in my schedule. Practical help is good and is absolutely part of living out the great commandment to love one another. But being the hands and feet of Jesus doesn't only look like handing out cups of water and giving the coats off our backs. It's grabbing a hand. It's bending a knee. It's pausing to pray with someone in the moment.

It's praying as we go on our way.

When Kathy and Margie stopped to pray for me, my immediate circumstances didn't change, but being seen by a sister and heard by

God made my burden feel lighter. Their words weren't ultraeloquent. Their prayers weren't elaborate. They didn't need to be.

Prayer has nothing to do with perfectly crafted sentences—it's about entering God's presence.

Prayer is the intersection of our obedience and God's faithfulness, our requests and God's power. This is why the writer of Hebrews invites us to "approach God's throne of grace with confidence, so that we may receive mercy and find grace to help us in our time of need."[6]

I felt so loved through the prayers of my friends. Being prayed for is one of the greatest kindnesses I've ever received. Some of the simplest prayers have made the most lasting mark on my heart.

We can be mark makers too.

Something powerful happens when we choose to listen carefully and then enter into someone's circumstances by taking their concerns straight to God. In moments like these, I know Jesus's words are true: "For where two or three gather in my name, there am I with them."[7] It's not about us. It's about Jesus. Any time we can point someone to Him? Help someone get a glimpse of His presence? A taste of His living water? There's no greater difference we can make.

If you've never considered the kindness of prayer, add it to the top of your simple difference list.

Let's be a friend like Kathy, a friend like Margie. Let's listen well and pray boldly. And this doesn't just pertain to a church-like setting. When you run into a friend at Target and can see behind the stiff smile that she's probably on the verge of a meltdown, stop and pray with her. When you see the glazed eyes of a stranger wandering the frozen food aisle, a weary mom at school pickup, or a stressed-out barista behind the counter, don't let awkwardness or timidity deter you from letting someone know they are seen—not only by you but by the God who made them and loves them.

Let's be people who risk feeling awkward for the sake of strengthening someone's faith—or maybe pointing them to Jesus for the very first time.

Want to be a helper, a come-alongside-er, a world changer, and a simple difference maker? Pray.

Pray first. Pray now. Pray continually.

• • •

When I think about the difference prayer can make, I think of a story my friend May Patterson wrote about a life-changing encounter she had—wait for it—in an airport. (What is it with airports? It's like God *really* wants us to understand this whole making a difference "as we go on our way" thing.) Whether we're seeking out opportunities to be kind and compassionate in Jesus's name or not, opportunities will come! And often with whom we would least expect.

This is May's story in her own words:

She barely made our flight. Just before the plane door closed, she charged in, marching down the aisle like a bulldozer. She wore a faded Def Leppard T-shirt, a puffy coat with a coffee stain, jeans that must've been two sizes too small, and a menacing scowl.

*Surely, she won't sit next to us,* I thought as I glanced at the empty seat next to my husband, Mike. But of course, she did.

She was as broad as she was tall, so it took her a while to wedge her body into the seat. Soon, another passenger came down the aisle behind her and said, "Lady, you're in my seat."

Angrily, she replied, "What in the 'heck' (or something like that) difference does it make? I'm not moving. Go find another seat!"

Meekly, the guy took a seat a few rows back.

*This was going to be a long flight.*

And it was, except we never left the ground. Snow began to fall. Not just light, happy snow, but fat, swarming flakes came down so hard that soon the ground of Salt Lake City Airport was covered, as well as the wings of the plane.

We had expected bad weather. The storm was so formidable it was even named "Snowstorm Helena," and now, we were stuck in it. We waited, fully loaded on the tarmac for over an hour.

We began talking with our new seatmate. She was a lady trucker. One of her kids was in jail, the other in rehab.

She said, "I married my current husband only because I was broke—not for love—and I told him this upfront." Then she rolled her eyes and said, "Here's the most ridiculous thing: my husband wants me to be faithful. That's impossible when I'm on the road."

*This was so much more than I wanted to know.*

Bitterly, she continued, "I'm not going to be faithful to someone I don't even love. He's such a loser. I've been on a cross-country haul and now I'm stuck in this 'dang' snowstorm. I have to get to Kansas City by tomorrow."

Then strangely, she teared up a little. Her rough, cursing-every-other-word exterior seemed to slip just a bit as she said, "I'm having gastric bypass surgery next week."

Fear flickered across her face as she grew nostalgic: "I've never really had a chance in life. Dad used to beat us kids when he was drunk. Mom died of an overdose. Basically, life sucks. Here's the tattoo I got last year after I was taken off suicide watch."

*I shuddered as I noticed the ferocious scar on her wrist next to her small peace symbol tattoo.*

After an uncomfortable silence, I redirected the conversation: "I hear gastric bypass is a life-changing surgery. It sounds like you've had a lot of pain in the past, maybe God will use this to give you a new life."

She narrowed her eyes at me defensively for a long minute. "That's pretty unlikely—since I'm an atheist," she snarled. "I believe God wants to make me as miserable as possible before I die. So far, he's done a 'heck' of a job."

Finally, our flight was canceled, so we deplaned. Later, I saw our seatmate walking in the terminal. For some reason I really can't explain, I felt compelled to stop and ask if I could pray with her about her upcoming surgery.

"It can't hurt," she grumbled.

So I prayed with a complete stranger, a lady trucker, an atheist, and a suicide survivor in a busy airport terminal in the middle of a snowstorm.

I don't do that very often.

In fact, I never do anything like that.

It felt awkward.

I didn't really want to do it.

"Lord, protect her life during surgery next week. Heal her pain. Give her a second chance—a fresh start, a new life that includes You as Lord. Let this be a new beginning. Show her that You love her and want to bless her. In Jesus's name, amen."

Tears flowed over her carefully built dam of brawn and bitterness. And my tears flowed too.

I cried because I realized how easily I avoid the people who need love the most.

It took being stuck in a snowstorm for me to stop and show compassion to a stranger. I wish it hadn't.

I held her as she sobbed for a long while. Finally, she whispered, "Maybe you're right; maybe God does love me, after all. Thank you." And then she walked away.[8]

I'm positive May never expected an ordinary flight to end in such an unexpected and extraordinary moment of prayer. No doubt her seatmate was surprised too.

When I first read this story, the stranger's raw confession of her recent plight and long-term struggles definitely startled me and kept me reading. But that's not why this story stuck with me. It marked my heart because May's willingness to listen to, pray with, and hold a stranger demonstrated the kindness of Christ.

• • •

Jesus was well known for taking an interest in those with rough edges and rougher pasts. There was an adulteress, a tax collector, and a criminal who hung next to Him on the cross. Jesus knew exactly what each of these people had done. While others judged and wanted to condemn them, Jesus took a different approach.

In John 8, we see the account of what happened when a group of religious teachers and Pharisees pulled a woman from the bed of a man who was not her husband. Talk about humiliating and awkward. They brought her to Jesus and intended to stone her to death in accordance with the law. But Jesus said, "Let any one of you who is without sin be the first to throw a stone at her." Eventually all her accusers dropped their rocks and left.

"Woman, where are they? Has no one condemned you?" Jesus asked.

"No one, sir," she said.

"Then neither do I condemn you," Jesus declared. "Go now and leave your life of sin."[9]

That's definitely not the outcome the woman was expecting. Can you imagine thinking you were about to face a painful death and instead encountering gentle mercy? Think of the mark Jesus's kindness left on her life. Surely that day cast a ripple of change.

In the book of Luke, we read the story of when Jesus wanted to stay at the house of a man named Zacchaeus. As the chief tax collector, Zacchaeus was notorious for his dishonesty and using his position to fatten his own purse while Jewish citizens faced poverty. A tax collector was seen as a traitor—loyal to the Roman government and its politics over the one true God. Zacchaeus was despised for it.

When Jesus entered Jericho, a crowd gathered to see the famous teacher. Zacchaeus also was desperate to get a glimpse of Jesus. But Zacchaeus was so short that he couldn't see over the crowd, so he ran ahead and climbed a sycamore-fig tree. "When Jesus got to the tree, he looked up and said, 'Zacchaeus, hurry down. Today is my day to be a guest in your home.' Zacchaeus scrambled out of the tree, hardly believing his good luck, delighted to take Jesus home with him."

The crowd was appalled that the highly esteemed rabbi would choose to be the guest of such a low and vile man. "What business does he have getting cozy with this crook?" Surely there wasn't a short supply of respectable hosts for Jesus and his companions. Of all the people in Jericho, why in the world would Jesus choose Zacchaeus?

But Jesus did not acquiesce to the crowd's judgment and indignation. Nor did Zacchaeus. Instead of crumbling under the weight of rightly earned social scorn, Zacchaeus decided to change. He promised to give half his income to the poor and to pay four times the damages if he was caught cheating. Then, in the presence of the crowd who questioned Zacchaeus's worthiness to associate with Jesus, Jesus made the most radical announcement of all: "Today is salvation day in this home! Here he is: Zacchaeus, son of Abraham! For the Son of Man came to find and restore the lost."[10]

He came to find and restore. Seek and to save. All people. Even a man like Zacchaeus.

Jesus didn't come for the cleaned up and pious. He didn't come for the faithful and esteemed. He didn't come for the tall or short, wide or slim, He came for all of us! He came to seek and save the lost.

To seek is the Greek word *zéteó*, which means search for, desire, require, or demand—universally and absolutely.[11] Do you hear the urgency and tenacity of Jesus's mission? He came to seek—*zéteó*—and save the wayward and missing and misguided. There's no doubt about it. Jesus is pursuing men and women. God's children who have wandered away or have yet to be found in the first place. It's the reason Jesus came! He declares it Himself.

But He's not just searching for and desiring to find us. He also came to save. To save is the Greek word *sózó*; it means heal, preserve, rescue.[12] Jesus was on a relentless rescue mission.

Have you ever needed to be rescued?

May's airplane seatmate did. The woman caught in adultery did. I sure have.

What kind of God cares enough about sinners to seek them out—in the middle of their muck—and pull them to safety? To chase after them with His love and saving grace? A God who is kind.

I am a sinner. You are a sinner. On our own we have nothing to brag about. But I will gladly borrow the words from Jeremiah 9:24 and let them echo loud:

> "But let the one who boasts boast about this:
>     that they have the understanding to know me,
>  that I am the Lord, who exercises kindness,
>         justice and righteousness on earth,
>             for in these I delight,"
>                 declares the Lord.

Have you ever considered how you have personally encountered God's kindness? Take a minute right now. Hold in your mind how you've missed the mark and how Jesus has met you there.

We cannot be simple difference makers by our own goodness or strength. We do not look to Jesus as a model so we can become mini saviors. There is only *one* Savior and He already lived and died and paid the ultimate price for our sins! Here and now, we get to recognize our depravity, drop our stones, and go—wherever God is asking us to go—with stories of how His radical love and kindness have marked us.

When we're faced with someone's sin—or even just their mess or stress or prayer request—judgment is the easiest choice. Thoughts creep into our minds: *I could handle that better. I would never do that. Get it together.*

If anyone has the right to judge, it's the sinless Son of God. But instead Jesus chose kindness. Compassion. Forgiveness. He didn't see the sexual sin of the woman or the greed and deceit of Zacchaeus or the sometimes-self-inflicted overwhelm of a college student or working mom. He saw people—broken and beautiful, loved by His Father—who get tangled in sin.

Jesus sees that living in sin is living death, so He offers people life instead.

Living the simple difference means pointing people to life with our prayers and kindness and open arms of acceptance.

May finished her story by writing,

Sometimes, God calls us to display His love to strangers. You may never know why. You may never see the outcome. It may feel awkward. You may not want to do it. But every time you let the Lord lead you to love someone who is hurting, you will walk away blessed. I sure did. Be willing to go to where the Lord sends you, today. Don't hold back. Demonstrate His love to the bitter, needy, and hurting.

Remember, there are souls at stake. People locked in misery. Truckers caught in a storm. They need to hear how much God loves them. So many people simply do not know. Tell them: "For God so loved the world (not as a mass, but as individuals, like you and me) that he sent his one and only son (which is the greatest gift of love ever given), so that whoever (truckers, atheists, travelers, writers) believes in him should not perish but have everlasting life" (John 3:16).

Amen and amen.

May our lives be prayers of thanks. May our words give testimony to God's amazing grace.

Let's invite the presence of Jesus and the power of the Holy Spirit to invade our lives and move through our circumstances. Let's live eyes wide open to the woman sitting next to us on the airplane and the man in the front pew at church. Let's be quick to grab a hand and bow our heads. Or hug a stranger and pray, eyes up to heaven.

The *how* of kindness through prayer doesn't matter. What matters is caring for another human enough to take their burdens to the Father.

I don't know if Kathy felt like it was an act of courage to pray for her college peer. I don't know if Margie thought she was making a difference by modeling intercession to a younger sister. But to me, they are women of impact, and the landscape of my faith is better because of them.

## *the simple difference*

**Pray it bold.**

*God, transform the way I think about prayer. In both the ordinary hum of life and intense moments of crisis, help me to remember that prayer is not the least I could do for someone but the kindest response. Teach me to pray in Your power. Help me to care more about others than my own fear or awkwardness. Make prayer a simple difference rhythm in my life. Use it to mark someone's heart today in a way I could never expect. Amen.*

**Live it now.**

- Listen closely to what someone shares today and then stop wherever you are and pray with them.
- Interact with someone you are not naturally drawn to (or whom you are naturally prone to judge). Show them the kindness of praying for them.
- Consider how you have personally encountered God's kindness. Write it down. Tell someone about it.

**Say it loud.**

Prayer is my best response, not my last resort.

*five*

# hardest at home

Sometimes I think it's easier to be kind to strangers than those we're closest to.

Sitting at The Coffee Bean & Tea Leaf tonight, I was happy to interrupt my writing to take photos for a group of strangers huddled around the big worktable with a box of cupcakes. But when I'm writing from home and my husband interrupts my concentration because he wants help with something small, I get ultra-irritated.

This weekend I was happy to give a fellow shopper my produce bag and stoop down to pick up the avocado she dropped. But when my kid drops his fork at the dinner table or wants another drink of water at bedtime, I feel put out by the inconvenience.

I didn't mind putting my phone conversation on hold when my neighbor came to the door and needed to borrow some olive oil. But get ready for dagger eyes anytime someone in my family taps my shoulder or has a pressing need while I'm on a call.

See what I mean about kindness at home?

Now sure, a passing moment with a stranger doesn't come with all the relational baggage and expectations of a family member or close roommate. But I recognize there's something wrong when I give the best parts of myself to a stranger but not to my husband and my kids. If you're single, divorced, widowed, or married without kids, this chapter applies to you too. You also don't have to share an actual living space in order to admit that there are people in your life who you are less likely to show intentional kindness to. Think about the way you talk to your sister on the phone or your level of irritation toward the guy who shares an office wall with you. The people whom we see the most or have known the longest often get the short end of the kindness stick.

My "warm and friendly, let me grab the door for you" persona in public doesn't always match my attitude and actions in private. I'm not exactly sure why this is, but the hypocrisy is starting to rub me raw.

I don't want to just put a Band-Aid on what hurts—I want to fix the point of friction.

In my first book, I wrote a chapter called "When the People You Love the Most Bring Out Your Worst."[1] It was about the surprising and shameful reality of anger in motherhood and how God didn't let me stay stuck there. I feel like this book might warrant a similar confession and exploration. We can call it "When the People You Love the Most Are the Hardest to Be Kind To." (I hope I'm not the only one who needs to read it.) Like my confessions of mom anger, sharing that it's hard to be kind to the people I hold most dear is not super fun to admit. I'm not proud of it. I mean, I pledged my life and heart to my husband. I vowed to love him in sickness and in health, for richer and for poorer—love in action no matter what. But when the guy's got the man flu or we don't see eye-to-eye on how to discipline our kids or we're stressed about money, it's easy to forget the part in the Bible that says love is kind.

The Bible doesn't water down how crucial love is above all else.

If I could speak all the languages of earth and of angels, but didn't love others, I would only be a noisy gong or a clanging cymbal. If I had the gift of prophecy, and if I understood all of God's secret plans and possessed all knowledge, and if I had such faith that I could move mountains, but didn't love others, I would be nothing. If I gave everything I have to the poor and even sacrificed my body, I could boast about it; but if I didn't love others, I would have gained nothing.[2]

No matter what you or I accomplish in a single day or in the scope of our entire life, no matter how impressive or influential, religious or sacrificial we are, if we don't show up and love the people in front of us, then all of our abilities and knowledge and good deeds mean nothing.

You might read these words and nod your head. But do you really believe them? Do you really live like it? Do I?

When I think about my kindness, or lack thereof, toward the people I love the most and wrestle with *why* it's sometimes hardest to live the simple difference at home, I come back to the ugly fact that I often elevate my own agenda, personal preference, and convenience over seeing others. Simply put, I put me over them. In small, everyday ways.

We're called to love our neighbors as ourselves, but it's easier just to love myself. Here's a picture of an ordinary way this recently played out:

My husband panfried dumplings for lunch, which is the most delicious way to eat them. Tender chicken and vegetables inside, chewy noodle wrapper with just the right amount of caramelized crunch outside. Yum! While Chris attended to the dumplings sizzling in the iron skillet, I prepped peanut butter sandwiches and apple slices for the kids and some yogurt and granola for me—an eclectic lunch trying to use up what we had on hand. We all devoured the strange and simple meal, enjoying each other's company as we passed dark dipping sauce and the final remnants of a bag of Chili Cheese Fritos.

Then Chris and I got into a fight.

Here's the gist of what happened. He started wiping down the stove from all the splattered oil (the only downside of panfrying) while I was rinsing milk cups and filling up the empty ice cube trays. Chris wanted me to take over cleaning the stove so he could go finish the garage project he started before lunch. But I wanted *him* to finish cleaning the stove because he was better at it than I was, and I needed to clean the rest of the kitchen. There was enough work in there for both of us, I not-so-gently pointed out. Back and forth we went. You clean the stove. No, you do it. (Please tell me I'm not the only one whose marital woes stem from mundane chores.)

If I would have just calmly explained to Chris that I really hoped he would clean the whole stove, things would have been fine. But instead I turned my request into a jab.

I said something along the lines of, "You should just finish it yourself, otherwise you're going to come back in and critique the job I did."

While there may be some truth to my statement, the way I said it wasn't helpful and it wasn't kind. There was an edge to my voice. I was being critical out of fear or expectation that my husband would be critical. *Umm . . . plank in your own eye, Becky.* My comment did not sit well with Chris. We had some more words. I wanted to play it off as being sarcastic. I mean, I wasn't outright nasty. My words weren't crude or overtly rude. But more often than not, sarcasm is just a socially accepted mask to cover unkindness.

And I had been unkind.

I wish I could have hit the slo-mo rewind button and watched my words retract back into my mouth like water into a bucket. But I couldn't. My husband was left dripping in the deluge of my unkindness.

Deep in my heart I desire to be kind to everyone, especially my husband. I'm sure you want to be kind to others too, with your loved ones at the top of the list. But sometimes there's a pile—or a mile—of junk on top of those good intentions that keeps us from acting kindly. Take a gander at this list of possible kindness blockers:

- fear
- defensiveness
- bitterness
- unforgiveness
- competition
- hurt
- sarcasm
- unmet (or likely unspoken) expectations
- disappointment
- anger
- grief
- irritation
- selfishness
- inconvenience

Any of these resonate with you? It's easy to see how our desire to be kind can get stuck in the muck. Now, with our boss or workout buddy or the produce guy stacking cantaloupes, it's easier to temporarily shove the pile of unresolved issues over to the side and let kindness rise. But with those we have a long relational track record? With our parent, sibling, child, spouse, or roommate? They get the realest real version of ourselves.

It reminds me of when my son Elias was younger. He would be an attentive listener and hard worker all day at kindergarten and then come home and completely unravel. Like, lose it. As his mom, I was his safety net, his comfort. But I was also first in line to receive his angry meltdowns, physical aggression, and verbal attacks. Yes, five-year-olds can have a lot of big emotions. But at school, my son was respectful and kind. I didn't blame my boy. He was young and immature and had a lot of growing up to do. He was learning to manage his emotions, learning to build stamina for good behavior at school and at home, learning to express himself with words instead of withdrawal or rage. The key word here is *learning*.

I'm thirty-nine but I obviously still have a lot of learning to do too. I'm guessing so do you. We've got to learn to identify the junk in our hearts and in our relationships that stifles kindness.

Here are a few questions that might help you recognize kindness barriers in your life and purpose to replace them with new patterns:

1. **Are you defensive and irritable when you're stressed?**

   Before you lash out at your brother or roommate, check in with yourself and assess what's really going on in your heart and mind. Go outside or light a candle. Take ten deep breaths. Pause for a minute and tell God about the burdens you're carrying and ask Him to carry them with you.

   Open your Bible or click the Bible App on your phone and read Matthew 11:28–30. We read that passage in chapter 3, but maybe you need to hear it again. Jesus says this, "Come to me, all you who are weary and burdened, and I will give you rest. Take my yoke upon you and learn from me, for I am gentle and humble in heart, and you will find rest for your souls. For my yoke is easy and my burden is light."

   Did you catch that? You get to *learn* from Jesus as He helps shoulder your load. What a word of hope and encouragement for whatever hard moment or season you're in.

Now share your feelings with your loved one and verbalize what's weighing you down—maybe there's a way they can help. Even if they can't, taking these steps to acknowledge your stress will empower you to choose a kinder response to others (and show that same kindness to yourself).

2. **Are you snappy or aggressive (or passive-aggressive) when you feel overlooked or underappreciated?**
It's easy to let bitterness build and resentment rise when you feel taken advantage of or taken for granted. But before cementing another block into your relational wall, ask yourself, Have I voiced my feelings to my loved ones? Have I modeled gratitude for my kids or shared with my spouse or close friend how much a word of thanks means to me?

These steps aren't automatic quick fixes, but they can help release some of your internal tension, which then frees you to show kindness regardless of what you receive in return.

Remind yourself of the truth that God is always mindful of you. While others may not notice or applaud your kindness at home, God sees it all. And receive this encouragement from Paul: "So let's not allow ourselves to get fatigued doing good. At the right time we will harvest a good crop if we don't give up, or quit. Right now, therefore, every time we get the chance, let us work for the benefit of all, starting with the people closest to us in the community of faith."[3] *Starting with the people closest to us.* Amen.

3. **Is sarcasm your default language? Do you dismiss people's feelings or carelessly cut with your words?**

Our tongues are powerful tools for building up (like we talked about in chapter 3), but they also can be used as weapons for tearing down. What is your default mode of communication? Do you listen to the feelings, wants, and needs of others with an openness to how you could help? Or is a dismissive remark or critical comment quick to roll off your tongue? Perhaps sarcasm is your brand of humor, which can come at the expense of showing authentic compassion.

Consider these words from Peter: "Summing up: Be agreeable, be sympathetic, be loving, be compassionate, be humble. That goes for all of you, no exceptions. No retaliation. No sharp-tongued sarcasm. Instead, bless—that's your job, to bless. You'll be a blessing and also get a blessing."[4] Write these words on a sticky note and post them where you'll see them. Let them sink into your heart. You don't have to change your personality, but you can let God change the way you speak to people.

• • •

Kindness doesn't mean you're a doormat. Being kind doesn't mean you don't train your kids to be independent and responsible. Kindness doesn't mean your spouse, roommate, or coworker shouldn't share the workload. Kindness never equates to allowing someone to treat you poorly.

But kindness *is* taking your own preference and convenience off the pedestal. Kindness is dismantling your own criticism and cynicism in order to pray, live, say, "How can I *be* the blessing in someone's day? How can I love my neighbor who happens to share my bed or live down the hall?"

Perhaps the kindness barriers I shared don't resonate with you. That's okay. Ask God to search your heart and reveal to you if there's anything keeping you from loving the people closest to you. If you're open to hear it, God will be faithful to speak it.

And all of us—regardless of our brand of struggle in this area—can take a good, long, fresh look at what love really means. If you're already familiar with the 1 Corinthians 13 definition of love, try to read these words as if it's for the first time.

Love is patient and kind. Love is not jealous or boastful or proud or rude. It does not demand its own way. It is not irritable, and it keeps no record of being wronged. It does not rejoice about injustice but rejoices whenever the truth wins out. Love never gives up, never loses faith, is always hopeful, and endures through every circumstance.[5]

When I hold this description next to a snapshot of my life, I'm sad to say the two pictures often don't look the same.

Kindness is not possible when you're being critical.

You cannot love someone when you're scrutinizing their actions.

I'm wiping tears as I write this because the realization is painful. It's a truth that's hard to swallow, like an oversized pill that you know is good for you, yet it chokes going down. I need more water.

Actually, what I need is more humility. More repentance. More genuine kindness.

Because kindness doesn't jab or overreact. Kindness isn't selfish or sarcastic. That day in the kitchen, the kind thing would have been to simply ask my husband for his help. Kind would have been to do the chore I didn't want to do in order to free up Chris to do what was important to him. Kind would have been to genuinely express my concern or feelings if I was worried about him critiquing my cleaning. Kindness is honest and open and others-focused.

Thankfully, seeing the discrepancy in how we're living and how we *want* to live is the first step toward making a change.

Home is our learning lab for living our one life well. How you treat the people you live with—or those you are in close relationship with—is either a glaring or gleaming indicator of the kind of mark you will make on the world. Mother Teresa is quoted as saying, "If you want to change the world, go home and love your family."

Perhaps how we treat people at home *is* how we leave our most important mark.

• • •

I recently came across a video on social media of a teenager named Keon asking his stepdad to adopt him on Father's Day. The young man read a letter in front of his family:

Dear Dad, where do I start? . . . You're my dad, my father, my OG, and my mentor . . . I thank God that you met my mom and did not give up on her or me. It takes a different kind of man to accept the responsibility that you did. You came into my life when I was wanting some change. If it was not for you, I promise you, I'd either be in jail or dead. You saved my mother and I. You blessed me with a happy life and four of the best summers I could have. Since day one you never left my side. Even when I got out of line, you never gave up on me.[6]

As the brave and vulnerable teenager broke down, overcome with emotion, I couldn't help but tear up too. What a beautiful testimony of what can happen when one person shows fierce love to someone in their home. Keon's stepdad made a lasting mark on his life. I can only guess that his impact looked a lot less flashy than a video gone viral and way more like showing up daily with kindness and compassion.

It probably looked like misunderstandings and hard conversations. It probably looked like offering continual encouragement and forgiveness. Continuing to love through frustration and disappointment.

I don't know all the details of Keon's story, but from watching four minutes of his heart poured out, I know without a doubt that his life is forever changed, because one man chose to love the people at home even when it was hard.

Kindness is not taking the easy way out by tuning out, checking out, bailing out. Choosing to love moment by moment, day by day, takes work. It's something we have to practice. But the people we love the most are worth the learning curve.

When I dream about changing the world through small, everyday acts of intentional kindness, I first think about where I go outside my home. How can I impact my neighborhood and community? How can those ripples of kindness create even bigger waves of change? I think about the opportunities I have to write and speak to broader audiences, to influence others through pages and on stages. But I would miss a huge arena for impact if I discounted loving the people in my home.

We would all be remiss if we dismissed the importance of loving the people in front of us—even when it's hardest.

Pastor and author Andy Stanley gave this encouragement: "Your greatest contribution to the kingdom of God may not be something you do but someone you raise."[7] Amen. Amen. Amen. And I'd add that it might be someone you pray for, sleep next to, or serve dinner to.

Take some time today to think about what loving the people closest in your life looks like. Put some everyday skin on your daily opportunities to be kind.

Learning to recognize opportunities to be kind at home is training your heart to love others over loving your comfort.

Here are some examples of what everyday kindness looks like for me:

- Kindness is tucking my growing boys in bed with a song and prayer (and listening to twelve more questions from Elias) even though they're old enough to put themselves to bed and I'd rather flop on the couch and watch Netflix.
- Kindness is getting a nightly snack for my husband (who is capable of cutting his own apple and scooping his own peanut butter) because he feels loved and cared for when I do it for him.
- Kindness is folding another load of laundry.
- Kindness is cuddling with my kids when I have PMS.
- Kindness is letting go of a grudge.
- Kindness is waiting till someone's out of the shower to flush the toilet or run the dishwasher.
- Kindness is sharing the last brownie.
- Kindness is looking up from my work to give attention to the son who wants to tell me every detail of his elaborate LEGO creation.
- Kindness is going to the store that has his preferred brand of milk.
- Kindness is giving the compliment.
- Kindness is cleaning the stove.

Kindness at home might sometimes feel hardest, but it's also the most ordinary kind of beautiful I know.

**THREE KEYS TO LIVING**

## *the simple difference*

### Pray it bold.

*God, I confess my critical spirit. I'm sorry for the ways I put my own preferences and agenda above loving the people right in front of me. The people in my home are a gift I don't want to take for granted. Bind my tongue when I'm tempted to let a jab or sarcastic comment fly. Help me to show up with kindness, moment by moment, day after day. Amen.*

### Live it now.

- Make your own list of what everyday kindness looks like in your home. Choose one (or more!) to do today.
- Pick one kindness barrier that resonates with you most and practice the new patterns of responding.
- Write out 1 Corinthians 13:4–7 and 1 Peter 3:8–9 on index cards or sticky notes. Post them where you'll see them most—bathroom mirror, kitchen cabinet, car dashboard—and read them every day.

### Say it loud.

Kindness is not possible when I'm being critical.

*six*

# kindness in crisis

My family cuddled on the couch, watching a movie as late-afternoon rain pelted down. It seemed fitting that there was a literal storm outside as the world stormed around us—the initial impact of COVID-19 was just getting serious in the US. Everything was shutting down. I only half heard my kids as they laughed at the characters onscreen and asked for a snack.

I kept thinking about our neighbor.

We've waved hello back and forth while pulling in and out of driveways dozens of times. When my boys were doing a Little League fundraiser, the white-haired woman generously donated twenty dollars. But beyond the fact that they always parked their black sedan in the garage, all I really knew is that the elderly wife and husband in the house catty-corner from us always brought in their trash cans on time and never had children. They had lived on our street longer than I've been alive, but their accent told of rich German roots. I wished I could remember her name.

I got up off the couch. "Whatcha doing?" my husband asked. He was home too. His work trip had been canceled, like most everything would be in the coming days.

"I keep thinking about those neighbors." I pointed diagonally out our front window. "I feel like I should go see if they need anything."

My husband agreed that was a good idea and told me to offer his help too. I pulled on my red rain shoes right over my fluffy socks. I didn't change out of my sweatpants or brush my hair. I just went. I popped up my umbrella, ran across the street, and rang the doorbell. After some time, my neighbor opened the door. "Yes?" she said tentatively. She didn't have on makeup either.

"Hi, I'm Becky. I live across the street. Over there with the three boys. And I was just wondering if you're okay. Everything is pretty crazy right now with the coronavirus, and I wanted to see if you needed anything."

"Oh, we're fine, Becky. But thank you for coming over and asking," she said, a shy smile spreading across her face.

I offered to run to the grocery store or the pharmacy anytime she needed. I told her my husband is really handy and would be more than happy to fix anything around their house. I asked her name. "Crystal," she said. "Like the glass."

I handed Crystal a handwritten card with our cell phone numbers and told her again to please call or text anytime. Then I popped up my umbrella again and walked back home.

Later that night, I called my sister while I was making dinner. I'm not a big fan of talking on the phone (introvert problems) and life is always busy for both of us, so we rarely talk. But as a kidney transplant survivor, my sister is immunosuppressed. I just felt like I should call. Unexpectedly, she picked up. "You were on my mind. How are you?" I asked while slicing croissants. My call was timely. It was good to talk.

The next morning I woke up thinking about a friend. I'd seen the memes flying around Facebook, heard about the racial slurs and suspicious looks darting toward anyone of Asian descent. I wanted to check in on one of my Asian American friends—I had a hunch she could use the reminder that she is wanted, loved, seen. I texted her. My hunch was right.

There was nothing big or extraordinary about any of the things I did. But each was a simple act of kindness that reminded me there is power in walking across the street, making a phone call, and sending a text. Reaching out and letting others know they are thought of makes a difference.

• • •

The idea for this book was birthed many years ago, after a stranger at the library said a few simple words of encouragement when I was having a hard time wrangling my three spirited boys and on the verge of a mommy meltdown. (I told that story back in chapter 3.) The kind comment made such a big difference in my day, I couldn't help but wonder how small acts of intentional kindness—like a few encouraging words—could impact the world. *Maybe I should write a book about that.*

Later, when I was in graduate school and working on my first book about motherhood, my kindness idea resurfaced. In my mind I started calling it the simple difference. I fleshed it out a little more, wrote it down, shared it with my mentoring professor. Then a couple of years after that, in a brainstorming session with (in)courage, the simple difference emerged again. It was at least another eighteen months later that those conversations turned into a book proposal, which eventually turned into a contract, which led me to actually transforming that long-ago idea into the book you're now reading.

Why am I inserting all of this backstory? Because now as I sit here in bed, writing about how every small kindness makes a big difference, my family and I are in the thick of COVID-19 quarantine. (No more writing in quaint coffee shops for me.) At the inception of the simple difference, never in a million years would I have imagined that our world would be reeling from a global pandemic. I have no idea what the world, or America, or my home state of California, or my beautiful city of Glendora, or my precious family—or yours—will look like on the other side of coronavirus, or if "the other side" will ever come.

But today I know more than ever that kindness matters. The way we treat the people inside our homes and as we go on our way is significant on every regular Monday—and especially in times of uncertainty and crisis.

I tell you the condensed version of this book's inception because I need you to know that the message in these pages is not part of some trendy be-kind bandwagon in response to what happened to the world in 2020 when COVID-19 changed life as we knew it. It's way more than that.

Yet I would be remiss to not call out recent global events, because this international crisis shines a spotlight on a timeless truth: Jesus "is before all things, and in him all things hold together."[1] At the beginning of the pandemic, life was especially crazy. Store shelves were empty. Medical supplies were scarce. Italy unraveled and China struggled to recover. Everything was canceled. Fear and anxiety were rampant. The unknowns were endless. And in the midst of it all, I saw God holding us together—through intentional kindness.

I saw it through my friend Joy.

Joy has a sister who is a surgeon at Saint Joseph Hospital in Denver. As the COVID crisis was beginning to build, so was the pressure over PPE (personal protective equipment). On March 18, 2020, over a family group text, Joy asked her sister, Dr. Jillian Ciocchetti, "How can we help?"

Her first request was for a reusable scrub cap and then a way to produce face masks. This wasn't just about personal provision for Jillian. There was a bigger desire to meet the large-scale need to get all healthcare workers the necessary equipment for their daily work.

"The seamstresses in our family jumped on it," Joy recalled. "A scrub cap was created and a design for a face mask was put together."

Simultaneously, another Saint Joseph's physician, Dr. Kelly McMullen, was designing her own mask. She had been warned that there weren't going to be enough masks and wanted to be proactive. Her design was almost identical to the one Joy's family created. So when Dr. McMullen caught wind of Jillian's project, she reached out and they joined forces.

With a collaborative effort from a group of ten friends and family members (including three doctors), a cloth mask was designed, made, improved upon, redesigned, remade (repeat). "One of my sisters built a website while I set up social media and email. I contacted media and boom—Operation We Can Sew It was born!" Joy explained.

Within one week of announcing the project, this small group of caring and concerned difference makers had almost 2,000 volunteers signed up to help sew. "It was overwhelming! People just wanted to do something—anything—to help and feel like they were making a difference."

Over the next sixteen weeks, Operation We Can Sew It gathered 5,514 volunteers who sewed close to forty-nine thousand masks that were distributed to over seventy-five different healthcare and community facilities including hospitals, homeless centers, fire departments, addiction treatment centers, clinics, and veterans groups. "Through the power of individuals coming together, using their talents and the resources they had on hand, we were able to make a difference in our community during a very difficult time for all of us," Joy said.

Operation We Can Sew It ended up making a tremendous impact in the lives of thousands of people! But it didn't start big. It started small. One sister sending a text. Several people seeing a need. A small group willing to sacrifice for the good of others. This is the simple difference in action, and it's beautiful to watch.

• • •

Fred Rogers famously said, "When I was a boy and I would see scary things in the news, my mother would say to me, 'Look for the helpers. You will always find people who are helping.'"[2] Social media isn't usually the first place I think to look for helpers.

Just scroll Facebook and you'll likely be bombarded with divisive messages from both sides of the political divide. Text-shouting and name-calling have become more common than pop-up ads. Commenters tearing down others from behind the safety of their device screens. No matter what the issue is, there always seem to be reckless and ruthless attackers poised at their keypads. There's a whole lot online to tempt us to lose hope in humanity. Yet when a crisis hits, the internet also provides a beautiful portal into the lives of good, kind, difference-making people.

In the wake of COVID-19, you didn't have to look far to find the helpers. My Instagram feed became a scrolling chronicle of kindness. Like Operation We Can Sew It, story after story emerged of how individuals were doing what they could with what they had right where they were. A landlord waived rent for his tenants. A popular blogger set up a spreadsheet for people in her online community to share their needs while others rallied to meet them. Kids armed with chalk took to the sidewalks, coloring rainbows and messages of hope and encouragement so that neighbors and dog walkers might remember that they weren't alone.

*Lord, as I go on my way, have Your way with me* has been our simple difference prayer. But what does that look like when physically going places totally changes? How is intentional kindness possible if we're no longer crossing paths with strangers at the ball game, meeting up with friends for dinner, or working side by side with colleagues? How do we make an impact if our daily path is primarily within the perimeter of our own property or the four walls of our apartment? Maybe these questions go through your mind all the time, not just in the face of quarantine and social distancing. If your mobility is restricted because of health issues, geography, or finances, you know how it feels when "going on your way" is limited.

One of the gifts—if we choose to see it—of times of crisis, seasons of transition, or unexpected circumstances is that they require us to think creatively about being kind.

I don't know what the world is like right now as you hold this book in your hands. But when schools and stores were closed, church was online, nonessential workers were working from home, and death and disease were rampant around the world—the power of small (and big) kindness was very much alive!

The helpers were helping. Ripples of the simple difference were making waves.

A story of kindness from my local Trader Joe's has been circling my city. As they frequently do, a checker asked a customer how things were going. The customer mentioned that a relative of hers in New York had just passed away from COVID. The checker excused herself and returned with a bouquet of yellow roses. The checker also asked the customer if she liked dark chocolate before grabbing some and adding it to her bag. Right where she was, this employee made sure the person in front of her knew that she was seen.

My friend Robin is an empty nester in Georgia. She baked sourdough bread and delivered a loaf along with a roll of toilet paper to every one of the eighteen homes in her small neighborhood. "It was a good excuse to get to know my neighbors," she told me. My friend Logan lives in South Carolina. She drove her two school-age sons to their old neighborhood, and they colored the walkway of their ninety-something former neighbors. Bright chalk in geometric squares is another way to remind someone who is homebound that you care.

Yes, a crisis can open our eyes to how much we belong to each other. Whether we live next door or across town, several states away or around the world, we can find simple, practical ways to love our neighbors well. I saw a post on Facebook about someone who gave an elderly neighbor, who lives alone, three pieces of colored paper: green, red, and yellow. If green is posted in the window, she knows all is well. Yellow means they need help, like an errand. Red signals an emergency. "Let's all look out for and help each other!" the post said.[3] Amen.

In Kansas, Danielle Garver and her daughter Addison made a simple difference in the lives of some residents in the Winfield Senior Living Community using a little time, creativity, and a roll of blue painter's tape. The mother-and-daughter duo created tic-tac-toe squares with tape on large windows, playing the simple game as they stood outside while residents pulled up wheelchairs on the inside.[4] The Garver girls didn't have any personal connection with the senior community. They just wanted to bring a smile to someone's face at a safe social distance.

These stories all share a common thread: use what you have where you have it.

Be creative. Be simple. Be bold. Be intentionally kind.

• • •

This sounds strange to say, but there are benefits to times of crisis. Crisis is clarifying. It helps you see what really matters. When the ordinary rhythms and security of our days are stripped away, it becomes easier to tune our ears to God's voice and arrange our lives in accordance with what He says.

"He has told you, O man, what is good; and what does the LORD require of you but to do justice, and to love kindness, and to walk humbly with your God?"[5] These words spoken through the ancient prophet Micah are *good* to be lived every day of our lives, but perhaps their impact is greatest when our need is greatest.

Consider these other unexpected upsides to being kind in times of crisis:

- Kindness requires taking our focus off ourselves and putting it onto others, which elevates our sense of purpose, peace, and calm in the midst of a storm.
- Kindness is contagious. Kindness inspires kindness. One small stone can yield multiple ripples.
- Kindness brings hope and comfort to the downcast and afflicted.
- Kindness helps us see the *imago Dei*—God's image—in each person.
- Kindness makes a natural disaster or pandemic personal.

A catastrophe moves beyond breaking news when you're sewing face masks for flesh-and-blood doctors who spend their lives saving others.

Friend, there is so much we cannot control in life. A reality I kinda hate. While we cannot fix a whole hard situation, we *can* be purposeful in using what we have, where we are, to do what we can.

I don't know if my neighbor will ever take me up on my offer to run errands or help with chores, but at least on a stormy day when uncertainty swarmed around us, Crystal knew that she was not forgotten. We can talk about what it means to love our neighbor. But a crisis will help us live it.

• • •

Obviously, crisis doesn't always mean a global pandemic. There are all sorts of circumstances that can put us in crisis mode. Sudden loss of a job or prolonged unemployment. A horrific accident or chronic illness. Death of a child, spouse, parent, or friend. Death of a business or dream. Betrayal. Natural disaster. Divorce.

Life is hard. None of us are exempt from struggle. Jesus Himself said it. "In this world you will have trouble."

But God's Son didn't stop there. Because crisis and hardship aren't the end of the story. "In this world you will have trouble," He said. "But take heart! I have overcome the world."[6]

When crisis threatens to crush us or someone we know or love, we can hold on to the assurance that our present pain and struggles won't always be this way. Even if suffering *is* our story for all our earthly days, we have another home and a greater hope beyond today! *This* is why we can take heart.

Jesus lived a perfect life and died as a sacrifice for the brokenness of the world. It's a central truth worth rehearsing and rehashing as many times as it takes to move from theoretical head knowledge into every-breath soul assurance. Jesus made meaning out of our troubles, rescued us from the grip of a fallen world, because of love. Understanding God's love for us is crucial to truly living out the simple difference—it's what both compels and equips us to love others.

Knowing that Jesus's life, death, and resurrection have ultimately conquered every crisis also puts our role in proper perspective.

We are not anyone's savior.

Repeat: it is not your job to save. But you can be a tangible reminder of the Savior's love to someone who is drowning in their circumstances or feeling alone in their pit.

You can be the one to say, "I'm sorry for your suffering" and then do something to love a friend or stranger in that place.

• • •

When someone we know is suffering or going through a crisis, it's easy to feel paralyzed by not knowing what to do or say; so we often default to doing nothing.

I know I have felt this way more times than I can count. A child dies. A husband leaves. The dream job gets taken away. The cancer comes back. And the little bit we have to give feels so insufficient, we worry that offering it will somehow do more harm than good. But here's what I've learned as both the giver and receiver of kindness in times of crisis: showing up always makes a difference.

You don't have to do everything—but you can do something. Put this truth on autoplay.

When my friend Courtney's one-year-old daughter, Quincy, stopped walking and was eventually diagnosed with a tumor wrapped around her spine—a rare and aggressive form of cancer—I didn't know what to say. How can anyone possibly find the right words or come up with an adequate gesture of support for a mom who is about to walk through the most horrific sixteen months of treatment anyone can imagine? What can someone possibly do for a parent who might hold their child for the last time? The answer is nothing. And everything.

Quincy's diagnosis was utterly devastating, and the course of her treatment, including dangerous surgery, chemotherapy, radiation, and immunotherapy, was completely daunting. But that wasn't the whole of Courtney's story. She also had five other children to care for.

Quincy was part of a set of girl triplets, with twin older sisters and one oldest brother. That's six kids ages seven and under when Quincy was diagnosed with cancer. Can you even imagine?

At the time, I didn't know Courtney super well. We went to the same church and Courtney had just joined the leadership team for our large moms' ministry. But my heart broke for this mama. I wasn't the only one. As a ministry team, we knew we couldn't rescue our friend from her grief or heal her baby or take care of all her kids during Quincy's many long hospital stays, but we could do something.

Another mom on our team had walked the brutal road of childhood cancer before. Krista knew how cold and lonely a hospital room could be, so she helped make a list of comfort items that could be helpful to Courtney. Everyone on the team pitched in. Warm socks, a fuzzy blanket, a journal, a devotional, nuts and granola bars and sweet snacks, sparkling water, gift cards, and cash. The large basket of items was thoughtful and beautiful . . . and it still felt like not enough.

Yet when Courtney walked into our friend Candace's house on her way between hospital and home, a small group of us were there, not only to deliver the basket but to open our arms and step into Courtney's grief. We cried and prayed and held our friend. We simply made space for her fears and tears. She was overwhelmed with gratitude for the basket but even more that we showed up.

Before Courtney left, another friend handed her a plastic container with homemade salad, figuring she probably hadn't really eaten. She hadn't. More tears for simple thoughtfulness and lettuce.

The simple difference is a powerful way of life as individuals. But there is something profound in the way kindness multiplies and the impact expands exponentially when people join hands and hearts to make a simple difference together. The way our moms' ministry team did that for Courtney and her family through Quincy's cancer will forever mark my heart.

For months we helped provide meals. We bought and wrapped Christmas presents for all six kids when there otherwise wouldn't have been any. We hosted a church bake sale to raise funds for Quincy's treatment that insurance didn't fully cover. No one swooped in, able to do it all. But ordinary women, with their own homes full of children and busy schedules and personal stresses, showed up and gave what they had. A double portion of spaghetti. A dozen blueberry muffins. Time to make a sign, decorate a table, wrap baked goods in cellophane. Simple acts of kindness born out of genuine love for another.

These things didn't speed up Quincy's treatment or take away Courtney's agony of watching her daughter be brought to the brink of death. Meals and money didn't ease a mama's guilt and sorrow over being away from her other five children for the good part of a year and a half. But Courtney would tell you that the prayers and tangible acts of kindness from friends and strangers made a huge impact in her family's life.

• • •

Perhaps you read a story like Courtney's and despite the tragedy of a baby with cancer, part of it also sounds like a bittersweet fairy tale you could never live. Maybe you're thinking, *What if I don't have a big village to band together with? What if I don't have friends or a church to rally help for someone going through a crisis? What if I'm just alone and it's too much for me on my own?* I hear you. As the saying goes, many hands make light work. But that doesn't mean you can't show up just as you are with just what you have and make an impact.

The simple difference isn't a mandate to meet every need. It doesn't require a certain kind of preexisting community. It's an invitation to listen to the Spirit of God and respond in love and kindness as He leads.

Here are twelve more simple ideas for loving well during a crisis:

1. Write a card and mail it. (Snail mail always brightens someone's day.)
2. Drop off games, puzzles, or toys you're not using.
3. Pick up the phone and call the person on your heart.
4. Leave homemade (or store-bought) brownies on someone's porch.
5. Just sit with a person in crisis. Be present in the pain or grief.
6. Ask a friend if you can pick up anything at the store you're already going to.
7. Deliver coffee or hot chocolate.
8. Offer a specific time to babysit to give a parent or caregiver a breather.
9. Make a batch of freezer meals and give them away.
10. Smile when others are angry, panicked, anxious, or rushed.
11. Offer to fold laundry, run an errand, or do the dishes.
12. Ask how someone is doing and really listen.

This list is just a jumping-off point, not a one-size-fits-all requirement. The only real requirement for living the simple difference is listening to the Holy Spirit and loving others however He leads you to.

Sometimes in the process, God will challenge you to expand the way you think about practical kindness.

There were many times that I opened an email asking for more meal sign-ups for Courtney's family and I just didn't have the capacity to help that week. But I didn't need to feel guilty for my limitations. When I had to say no to bringing dinner, I could say yes to showing my friend I loved her in another way. For me, this often looks like offering words.

I've got a lengthy text history to Courtney, full of Scriptures and prayers and just small reminders that she and her family are not forgotten on the long haul of a prolonged cancer journey.

Sometimes we stumble against unspoken barriers to offering the kindness of encouraging words in times of crisis: uncertainty and insecurity. They sound like this:

*I don't even know where to start.*

*What if my words sound trite?*

*What if I say the wrong thing and offend them?*

*What if I make their pain worse?*

Thoughts like that have crept into my mind many times. You too?

In some ways those thoughts are rooted in a valid concern. I'm sure we could fill a whole chapter with stories of how someone's well-meaning words actually did more harm than good. But here's what I've discovered: saying something is worth the risk.

Start by acknowledging that your words fall short. Acknowledge that you're not trying to fix their pain. This gives freedom to you and to the person in crisis to know the limits of your encouragement or gift. Then give it anyway.

I recently found out that a friend lost her baby. I was devastated for her. What could I possibly say to ease her pain? Nothing. But I could let her know that she is seen. That her sorrow is shared. That she is loved in the midst of the unbearable.

As I wiped my tears, I put together a little collection of gifts I had on hand. A candle. A journal. A card scrawled in my sloppy penmanship with my sincere prayers. I dropped the gift on my friend's porch. It wouldn't bring her baby back but perhaps she would feel a tiny bit less alone in the grief.

Later I got a text message that said, "Becky, my son just brought in your sweet gift and most amazing card with such words of wisdom.

Thank you! I am feeling so down today, words cannot express how thankful I am for a friend who cares so much."

I'm so glad I followed that nudge to move beyond my sad feelings and love my friend in action. There are *plenty* of times I have not been so attentive or willing. It's easy to have a thought enter our mind or prod our heart, but then we overthink and second-guess it. We hesitate until that spark of kindness is snuffed out by inaction or blown away by the breeze of distraction.

In order to live the big impact of small kindness, we have to pay attention, both to the people around us and to the Spirit within us.

In his second letter to Timothy, Paul reminds us, "For the Spirit God gave us does not make us timid, but gives us power, love and self-discipline."[7] Our timidity can rob the world of the love and kindness God wants to show others through us. Don't let it.

When crisis hits, be the person who shows up for another. Pay attention to the needs around you. Offer what you have. Do it imperfectly. Do it afraid. Let love cast out your fear.

## THREE KEYS TO LIVING
### *the simple difference*

**Pray it bold.**

*God, in times of crisis, I want to be a helper. I know I'm not a savior, but I believe You can use simple acts of kindness to make a big difference in the life of someone who is hurting. Give me courage to offer what I have even when it feels so small. Thank You that You've already overcome the world! Help me to love others as we still slog through today's brokenness. Amen.*

**Live it now.**

- Walk across the street or hallway and check on a neighbor, or text the person you're thinking about, even if it feels out of the blue.
- Dial the number of someone who you know is struggling or grieving and just hold space for their voice.
- Show up with a meal, a hug, or an imperfect basket of love for someone going through a crisis.

**Say it loud.**

Showing up always makes a difference.

*seven*

# undeserved

It was a Sunday morning, and my house resembled a scene from the classic Warner Bros. cartoon *Looney Tunes*. But instead of one Tasmanian Devil whirling around in chaotic mayhem, I had three. My very own *tornado of tiny testosteronies*, as I liked to call my boy crew. A term dripping with both affection and exhaustion.

My husband was working out of town, and I just wanted everyone to stop whining, find your shoes, quit poking your brother, and GET IN THE CAR so we can go to church! Maybe my kids weren't the only ones who looked a bit like Taz.

Eventually I got my three littles strapped in the minivan—we were only eight minutes late, and I was only slightly sweating. Thankfully the drive to church was short.

Our historic church is beautiful with its nearly one-hundred-year-old cobblestone exterior and dark oak beams spanning the sanctuary. But the parking lot also has "character" reflecting the age of the church. It boasts a whopping twelve spaces. The congregation tries to save those prime spots for visitors and seniors, which means at least a hundred other families at each service scour the surrounding neighborhood for a place to park. Our late arrival wasn't helping.

"Keep it down, please," I called in a not-so-pleasant voice to the squirmy boys behind me as my eyes darted down narrow side streets. Both sides of every street were packed. Then, to my surprise, I spied a gap between two cars near the church entrance. I glanced at the clock, ten minutes after eight. *Why did I think early service was a good idea? At least we should still make it in for half of the worship*, I thought, whipping into the open slot along the curb. Then, crash. Crunch. The horrible sound of metal and hard plastic scraping together.

I hit the car behind me.

Instantly hot tears stung behind my eyes.

"Mommy, what was that sound? What happened? Did you crash, Mom? Did you break the car? Mom, did we just get in an accident?"

"PLEASE be quiet!" I yelled. I squeezed my eyes closed and put my head down on the steering wheel. *How did this happen?*

But I knew how it happened. I pulled in nose-first and cut the angle too close, clipping the car next to me. It happened because I'm afraid of parallel parking. Sometimes the pull-forward, back-it-in method works great on the first shot and other times it turns into a seventeen-point turn, and I just wanted to get to church! It happened because I was frenzied and rushing and my patience was unraveling and so was the peace of Jesus (or my awareness of it).

"Boys, *stay* in the car. I will be right back."

I climbed out of the van and walked to survey the damage. I wasn't concerned about my fifteen-year-old, prone-to-overheating, crumbs-embedded-in-booster-seats minivan. We bought it with several dings and the odometer already past one hundred thousand miles. But the car that I hit wasn't as well used. No, it was a new SUV with shiny red paint whose front bumper I had left a sizable dent in.

I snapped a few pictures of the damage. Tears now rolled down my cheeks as fellow church stragglers strolled by on the sidewalk. I tried not to make eye contact. My kids sounded like caged monkeys.

Back in the van I scrounged through my bottomless purse looking for a pen and paper. All I could find was my Walmart shopping list and a green crayon.

"*Please,* boys! I need you to keep it down. I'm trying to think."

"What's wrong, Mommy?" one asked, seeing the tears I couldn't hold back.

"I'm just mad at myself, and I feel sad that I accidentally hit another car. I'm writing a note to say sorry and so the owner can call me and I can pay for the damage to their car," I explained.

I looked at my reflection in the rearview mirror and tried to wipe away the black mascara streaks under my eyes.

"Okay, boys. Please get out and stand quietly right by the van."

I tucked my green-crayon–written note under the red car's windshield wiper blade. I hoped my explanation, apology, and contact info were legible. I dropped the boys off at their Sunday school classes and finally slinked into the back of church. I left my sunglasses on. I squeezed past a crowded row of singing folks and found one open seat next to my friend Kyan.

"Hey!" she whispered over the worship song. "So good to see you! How are you? Chris traveling?"

I hugged my sweet friend and couldn't hold back the tears. I hung my head, pressed down by the weight of shame.

"Oh, no! What's wrong?"

I leaned in close and confessed my collision and how stupid I felt and how I was worried about telling Chris and what it would cost and how I yelled at the kids and maybe I should just go home. Ky squeezed my hand and told me everything would be okay. She fished a tissue out of her diaper bag.

I'm sure I'm not the only person who has ever had a parking mishap. Accidents happen. That's what I would tell a friend. But that didn't help the sick feeling in my gut, because I should have prevented it. The accident was one more thing in a long line of recent mess-ups. Lost insurance card. Overdue library books. Broken vacuum. Forgotten grapes and zucchini rotting in the refrigerator. Chapstick melted in the dryer because I didn't check the pockets—lasting stains to remember. Thank-you cards never sent. Shattered relationship.

I felt like a constant disappointment.

After church I texted my husband pictures of the dented red car. He was pretty sure the whole bumper would need to be replaced. "This new kind of material doesn't really get patched or repaired. They will require a whole new one. It'll probably cost $800–1K," he texted back.

A fresh lump lodged in my throat. I couldn't swallow.

That afternoon and into the evening, my heart raced every time my phone buzzed or rang. I panic-checked my text messages for days. If a call came in from a number I didn't know, I let it go to voice mail, too scared to talk to the person whose car I had hit. Yet I was also desperate for the confrontation to just be over with. But the red car owner never called.

A week or more passed. What if the wind carried my note away? What if the owner saw my van and knew it was me and thinks I'm a jerk? The what-if scenarios swirled in my head, along with a steady stream of low-grade anxiety.

Then one day my phone rang. Without thinking I answered. "Hello?"

"Hi, is this Becky? This is Mary. I go to Cornerstone Bible Church."

The voice clearly belonged to an elderly woman. My fragmented mind tried to place her.

"I'm sorry it's taken me a while to call you," she continued. Suddenly the puzzle pieces locked into place, and the image of her damaged red bumper flashed in my mind. But before I could stammer out my apology, she went on. "I just wanted to call and say thank you for your wonderful note. It was so very kind of you to leave that for me. And I just wanted to call and tell you how much I appreciated it."

"Umm. . . ." My mouth was dry, but my eyes were not. "Well, it was the very least I could do. And I am so sorry I hit your car, Mary. Should we talk about repairing the damage?"

"Oh, not at all, dear. I could barely see a scratch. It's just fine. Not to worry. I only called to tell you thank you for your thoughtful little letter. I hope you and your family have a wonderful day."

I tried to protest, to make very sure I couldn't fix the damage. But all Mary kept saying was "Thank you for your kindness." And all I could stammer through my tears was the same. "Thank you for your kindness."

I hung up in shock.

Why would a stranger do that?

I reasoned out potential answers. Maybe Mary's eyesight wasn't so keen. Maybe her sparkling new car didn't mean that much to her. Maybe she had loads of money to fix or replace it. Perhaps she remembered what it was like to be a frazzled mom who accidentally left the milk on the counter to spoil and occasionally got into a fender bender. These scenarios are possible. Or perhaps Mary saw my Sunday morning parking failure as an opportunity to offer a measure of what she's already received in full—lavish, undeserved kindness. The kindness of being eternally loved and forgiven by Jesus, compelling her to pass on a dose of unmerited favor.

In the wake of my relief over having the financial consequences of my actions waived, I was consumed with a fresh awareness that undeserved kindness is hard to accept—and brave to give.

But really, is there any other kind?

• • •

When I think about how Jesus demonstrated the power of unde-served kindness, two stories come to mind. The first is a story He lived. We looked at it back in chapter 4—the story of the woman caught in adultery. As you'll remember, the prevailing Jewish law at the time required that the punishment for such an act was death by stoning. This is what the men who dragged the woman from her lover's bed believed she deserved. But Jesus gave what was *undeserved*—mercy, a chance to change, a fresh start. If you ever find yourself questioning the kindness of God or how He calls us to show kindness to others, go back and read John 8.

The second is a story Jesus told. You might be familiar with it; it's often called the story of the prodigal or lost son.

It all started when a group described as tax collectors and sinners was gathering to hear Jesus teach. A bunch of Pharisees and teachers of the law were complaining about Jesus's track record of keeping company and eating with those they labeled "sinners." In response, Jesus told three parables—simple stories used to illustrate spiritual lessons.

The story of the lost son goes like this: A father has two sons. The older son is hardworking and faithful and obeys his father. The younger son demands his inheritance early and goes off and squanders his money on prostitutes and "wild living." He eventually finds himself destitute, eating less than the pigs he is tending in a foreign country. Desperate and ashamed, the son decides to go back home and beg his father to let him work for him to earn his next meal.

But the son never gets a chance to grovel for forgiveness or plead his case. His dad sees him from far off and runs to him. The son doesn't get scolded; he gets embraced. Wrapped in his father's arms.

Without hesitation, the father plans a huge celebration! He asks a servant to bring his son a robe, sandals, and a ring. And to prepare a fat calf—tonight they will feast in the most lavish way.

Then the other son comes—and questions it all. Why would his father reward such reckless, dishonoring behavior? Why would his brother, who squandered their shared wealth and literally stank like swine, be treated better than he, who had done everything right?

(As a mom of three sons, I know this fight for fairness well. As a person, I know the burning desire for equity. We want good behavior to be rewarded and bad behavior to be punished. Anything that deviates from this logical reaction is just plain wrong. Right? Not so much, according to Jesus.)

The father's reply to his "golden boy" says it all. "'My son,' the father said, 'you are always with me, and everything I have is yours. But we had to celebrate and be glad, because this brother of yours was dead and is alive again; he was lost and is found.'"[1]

Death to life. Lost to found. In God's sight, these are the reasons we should throw a party!

Did the irresponsible son deserve a lecture? Should he have been forced to live with the natural consequences of his actions? Was it reasonable to require him to earn back his broken trust by working in the fields? I think both brothers would agree with a resounding yes.

But this story isn't about what's deserved. It's about God's radical love for His kids who mess up.

Let's say it again loud so that it reaches the dark and unbelieving corners of our hearts: the love of God is revealed in undeserved kindness toward His people.

Giving what is undeserved is central to the gospel message and the saving grace Christ offers.

Jesus's parable doesn't tell us how the lost son reacts to his dad's surprising kindness. But there's not a whisper of doubt in my mind that it made all the difference in his life.

When we truly know the kindness of God, we can run with joy to heap it on others without hesitation.

• • •

I grew up on flannelgraph Bible stories and grape juice communion cups. When I was five years old, I accepted Jesus as my Savior—while sitting on the toilet. It's a good place to think. I prayed the prayer I'd heard in Sunday school and flushed the potty along with my sins. I washed my hands and believed with my whole heart that God had washed all of me clean. I went downstairs and told my mom my porcelain-throne testimony. Today there's nothing I love more than talking to people about Jesus.

Yet even though I've called Jesus Savior for almost my entire life, even though I've gone to church for nearly four decades and read my Bible regularly for the last twenty years, even so—the thing that has helped me truly understand the depth of God's loving-kindness and grace wasn't a sermon or theological discussion. It was a lady named Mary calling to say I didn't have to fix her banged-up bumper.

I know the words of Romans 5:8 well. "But God demonstrates his own love for us in this: While we were still sinners, Christ died for us." This verse sums up the power and beauty of undeserved kindness in the greatest display ever made.

Undeserved. That's the undercurrent of God's great story of redeeming His people. He did what He did not have to do for the sake of love.

I know I don't deserve the love of God. And yet, if I'm honest, I forget this crucial fact. I take God's love for granted. It's so ingrained in who I know Him to be and who I know I am as God's daughter that it's like, "Of course Jesus died on the cross for my sins. Of course God loves me unconditionally. Of course He's going to lavish me with blessings." Yikes.

I don't begrudge my Sunday school upbringing. I know it's a gift to inherit a lineage of faith. It's a special protection to be acquainted with Jesus since I was a little girl. Rougher pasts and edgier testimonies don't make a better Christian. But I think there can be an advantage for those who have squarely faced the death and desperation that come from being undeniably entangled in sin and living apart from God: clear recognition of their undeniable need for a Savior.

I have a friend whose story holds many heartbreaking chapters. Her list of destructive life patterns is long. The choices she made in the past break her heart too. But even more, my friend breaks over the crazy, unimaginable, totally undeserved kindness of God in her life. He literally saved her from the self-imposed brink of death. Again and again. He healed relationships she had shattered. He infused hope in hopeless situations. He pulled her from the pit of despair and called her loved.

I've seen my friend respond with extravagant kindness to people who have deeply wronged her. Almost to the point that I'm like, "Umm, maybe they deserve your bitterness or contempt or a flat-out punishment." (I promise I'm a good friend and not a total jerk.) At first glance I don't always understand my friend's reactions or perspective. But then I think about the degree to which she is aware of God's unmerited favor in her life and it clicks: she wants other people to know her Redeemer.

It's like she's quoting Scripture with her life: "Don't you see how wonderfully kind, tolerant, and patient God is with you? Does this mean nothing to you? Can't you see that his kindness is intended to turn you from your sin?"[2] I love the way The Message version expresses that last phrase: "In kindness he takes us firmly by the hand and leads us into a radical life-change."

I hear the words of Luke 6:35 in my friend's actions too: "But love your enemies, do good to them, and lend to them without expecting to get anything back. Then your reward will be great, and you will be children of the Most High, because he is kind to the ungrateful and wicked."

God is kind to the ungrateful and wicked. That's you. That's me. That's the person who rear-ends you and who says that nasty thing to you. That's the coworker who steals your sandwich out of the break room fridge. That's the neighbor who knocks over your trash cans and the boy across the street who whacks a baseball into your upper window. It's the person who cheated you, abused you, snubbed you, and snaked your front-row parking spot. That is who God is kind to. That is who we have the daily, on-our-way opportunity to be kind to too.

I know this is way easier typed than lived. But if we want to be difference makers in this world, if we want to change the trajectory of someone's life through simple, brave, intentional acts of kindness, then we must follow God's lead and love others when it's undeserved. No doubt it will take courage and humility. No doubt it will be worth it.

I wrecked Mary's car. Her kindness wrecked me in the best possible way. And in the process, she pointed me back to Jesus.

## THREE KEYS TO LIVING
### *the simple difference*

**Pray it bold.**

*God, thank You for showing me the ultimate kindness that I didn't deserve by giving Jesus to pay the debt for all my sin. Help me to not forget it! I want to actively look for ways to love others like You do. Provide a way for me to make a lasting mark on someone's heart by doing the unexpected, undeserved thing. Amen.*

**Live it now.**

- Instead of demanding that the one who wronged you make it right, offer the mercy of undeserved kindness.
- The next time someone does something rude or out of line, choose to respond with a smile and kind word.
- Memorize Romans 5:8: "But God demonstrates his own love for us in this: While we were still sinners, Christ died for us."

**Say it loud.**

Offering undeserved kindness leaves a lasting mark.

*eight*

# where your feet are

My husband is a college volleyball coach. He often reminds his athletes to be where their feet are. Sometimes he'll notice a player is on the court participating but she's not really present. She's thinking about the term paper she has to write or the exam she needs to study for. She's replaying that fight she had with her roommate or rehearsing how she's going to ask her boss for a raise or contemplating what she's going to wear out on Friday night. *Be where your feet are* means be in the moment, on the court, engaged in the play, aware of your teammates. Be present not only in body but fully in mind and heart too. It's a necessary posture and mindset for athletes who need to be attentive, active, and ready to react, from their fingertips to their toes.

And it's a necessary mindset for all of us.

The other day my family was on a hike in our local San Gabriel Valley foothills, one of our favorite activities. As a family we love listening to crickets chirp and songbirds sing. We love spotting a busy woodpecker pecking perfect holes high up in a tree. We love the sound of the breeze rustling fallen leaves and water babbling over round stones, thankful for running water in a riverbed that's often California bone-dry.

The trails are quiet and peaceful, save for nature's melodies and our huffing breath giving testimony to a steep incline. Oh, and of course, Elias's voice.

Elias is my very sweet, inquisitive, and *loud* middle child. He's ten and has been asking nonstop questions since the moment he learned to talk. As a toddler it started with the incessant *why?* Over the years it's morphed into more sophisticated, complex, and random question-asking. This is part of what makes Elias awesome. His mind is always working, turning, spinning in a hundred different directions. He's a verbal processor, so he says what he sees and asks questions as a way of experiencing the world around him. But it's also really hard for Elias to be where his feet are.

Focusing in school is challenging for him. When playing baseball or soccer he's more likely to catch a ladybug or watch a hawk soaring above than remember to keep his eye on the ball and listen to his coach. For all of Elias's amazing qualities—compassionate, resourceful, entrepreneurial, brave—he often fails to hear the person who's speaking to him three feet away or see the socks right under his nose.

So we're never surprised (though slightly irritated at times) that Elias spends our peaceful family hikes talking—the whole time. He's got questions about housing prices and the stock market. He wants to know what kind of cabin or mansion he should build next in Minecraft and do I think he should use blue glass blocks or clear. He's got questions about the movie we watched last night and what kind of airplane will we fly in four months from now on our first out-of-state family vacation. Meanwhile he trips on a rock and nearly whacks his brother in the head with the large stick he's carrying. "I didn't mean to, Mom! I just didn't see him."

We take three silent steps. "What's for dinner? Who built this trail? What do people spend their money on? Did my great-grandpa fight in World War II?"

And on and on and on until finally Chris says: "Elias, be where your feet are!"

"What?"

Father turns to son and we all stop on the trail to listen to the lesson.

"Elias, you are thinking and talking and asking questions about so many different things that you're missing the beauty all around you. You almost poked your brother's eye out with that stick because you weren't paying attention. Your feet are right here, in this canyon, on this trail. Be right here. Practice just quietly noticing what's right in front of you."

We miss the beauty (and can potentially harm others) when we don't live in the moment and pay attention to our surroundings.

*Be where your feet are* isn't just sound advice for a competitive athlete or distractible child. It speaks to the key of living the simple difference—and the part that I often fail so miserably at.

As much as I don't want to admit it, *I* am highly distractible. In my mind I'm usually working on a writing project, thinking about a friend I want to check in with, rehearsing a conversation I need to have, and planning dinner all at the same time, while standing in line at the grocery store. Oh, and I might also be simultaneously checking Instagram.

I tell myself this mental hamster wheel is just how I'm wired. I label it *productive*. But in reality, rather than helping me further my goals, it's a perpetual cycle that often prevents me from being available to people.

Choosing to *not* be where my feet are means choosing what's in my head over who's in front of me. The same is true for you, friend.

When we're absorbed in our thoughts, we simply do not have the capacity to also be fully aware of God and others. When our focus is turned inward, we won't be ready to respond outward.

I can start my day by praying, *Lord, as I go on my way, have Your way with me.* But if I follow up that prayer by scrolling Facebook on my phone while waiting for my kids at school pickup, and then rehashing my mental list of worries and to-dos while taking in the trash cans or walking into church or talking with a coworker, chances are high I'm going to miss God's answer.

On the flip side, go back and look at the examples of living the simple difference in this book. Think back to the times a kind word, sincere prayer, generous gift, or small encouragement from someone at just the right time has made a meaningful difference in your life. Would those moments of impact have been possible if the person who showed you kindness was distracted? We have to be where our feet are to see people.

I know I have missed opportunities to show the kindness of Christ because I failed to be mentally present. Probably too many times to count. And I can't even tell you when or how or what was lost because I wasn't aware enough to notice. Is the same true for you? From what I observe in our increasingly device-addicted, don't-make-eye-contact world, I'm not the only one who struggles.

So how do we change this?

I'm tempted to believe that my mental hamster wheel is inevitable—just a programmed part of me. Mind constantly spinning. Thoughts, ideas, and feelings in perpetual motion. When I'm out in public running errands or sitting at the dinner table with my family, I'm aware of my own wants, needs, worries, and emotions. It's easy to go through life swirling in my own self-focused bubble. Can you relate? Or maybe you're like my Elias and you're a curiosity junkie wrapped up in the next ten questions. Or maybe for you, living distracted looks like living numb. Or living cynical. Or living critical.

We've all got a propensity to rely on whatever default serves ourselves best. Not that we're purposely or even consciously selfish. But if "that's just how I am" has ever been your reason for not being present, for not being willing or able to see and serve others first, then it's time for a reboot.

We can't be simultaneously absorbed with self and aware of others.

So what does rewiring our default settings look like? It looks like intentionality and repetition. We can't master being mentally present on a single occasion. It's a continual choice. A posture we have to choose each day, in each new situation and place.

Here are nine simple strategies to help train your body and mind to be where your feet are:

1. **Name your distractions.** How are you wired? What keeps you from being present? Identify it so you can deal with it.

2. **Pray.** *Lord, help me be fully in this moment.* God's not surprised by how you get sidetracked, numb out, or turn inward. Rely on His strength to change.

3. **Take five deep breaths.** When your mind is all over the place, slow breathing helps bring your focus back to the present.

4. **Put your phone away.** You only have one set of eyes. You can't give yourself to the people around you if you're absorbed in the screen in front of you.

5. **Attune your senses.** What do you see, hear, smell, taste, or feel? Being physically anchored to the moment will reduce your stress level and heighten your awareness.

6. **Enjoy the art of people watching.** Do nothing but notice the people in proximity to you—not with a critical eye but with a curious love. How has her day been? What is his story? What might she be thinking? Being interested in and attentive to the people around you primes your heart for a compassionate response.

7. **Write down your to-do list, worries, or prayer requests.** Get them out of your head and onto paper so your mind has freedom to be where you are.

8. **Notice what's happening around you.** Beyond who you see, look for what need you could meet. Is there trash on the ground? Does someone need a hand with the door? Has a child lost his way? Is someone sad, hurting, angry, being treated unfairly? Pay attention so you can be ready for action.

9. **Just be.** Right where you are. When you stop speaking, spinning, striving, or desensitizing, you'll be able to hear God's still small voice and receive His great big love. You need both to live the simple difference.

Adapt this list to fit your individual personality, struggles, and circumstances. If you were one of my husband's athletes, you might listen to a set playlist of songs while you warm up to get your mind focused on the practice or game ahead. If you're like my inquisitive son, you might set a timer for ten minutes and practice not talking, only listening. If you're a multitasking junkie like me, you might rehearse the mantra, "People over productivity," and create boundaries for work and nonwork hours.

There's no perfect formula for this. But there is one perfect example we don't want to miss.

• • •

As I stumble through life like my kid on the trail preoccupied with his questions, I remember the words of Paul to the Philippians: "Do nothing out of selfish ambition or vain conceit. Rather, in humility value others above yourselves, not looking to your own interests but each of you to the interests of the others."[1] And here we find simple difference barrier #47: valuing ourselves above others. Okay, we're not actually numbering them or keeping track, but when I consider how Jesus lived and His desire for us to follow in His people-loving, others-centered footsteps, I know I'm bound to trip.

But tripping doesn't mean the journey isn't worth it. I'd rather falter and fall while following Jesus than skip on my merry way alone and one day realize my path has led nowhere but to more of me.

Paul's instruction to look to the interests of others is immediately followed by these words: "In your relationships with one another, have the same mindset as Christ Jesus."[2] What is that mindset? The Message version explains it like this:

> He had equal status with God but didn't think so much of himself that he had to cling to the advantages of that status no matter what. Not at all. When the time came, he set aside the privileges of deity and took on the status of a slave, became *human*! Having become human, he stayed human. It was an incredibly humbling process. He didn't claim special privileges. Instead, he lived a selfless, obedient life and then died a selfless, obedient death—and the worst kind of death at that—a crucifixion.[3]

In other words, Jesus, who was fully God, came to earth as fully human. He stayed connected to the Father in spirit, but in mind and body, He was concerned with what was right in front of Him. This was a thirty-three-year-long exercise in being fully present. Jesus let His human form direct His human response. He chose to be—in His presence, purpose, and posture—where His feet were. On earth. And Jesus's life demonstrated what love looks like. Selfless obedience. Putting others first.

Jesus didn't have to humble Himself through physical birth and brutal death. He chose to. For us.

So how do we take on the mindset of Christ that elevates the value of others? How do we make our daily posture like His? *Love*—it's the not-so-secret sauce of living the simple difference.

Jesus said, "Greater love has no one than this: to lay down one's life for one's friends."[4] Of course, He was talking about His own great love for us.

The apostle John reminds us that this kind of love-in-action wasn't intended just for Jesus. "This is how we know what love is: Jesus Christ laid down his life for us. And we ought to lay down our lives for our brothers and sisters."[5] Jesus set the example. We get to follow.

Okay, so you might be wondering how this all connects. How did we go from a college volleyball pep talk to an overly talkative kid on a hike to a mental hamster wheel and Jesus's crucifixion? (And just get ready, we're headed to a banana story next.) The connecting thread is woven with the fibers of being mentally engaged and actively present.

We cannot do the work God wants us to do or be the people He wants us to be if we're checked out from what's going on right in front of us. Period.

• • •

Want to live your life on purpose? Want to make a mark on humanity—one human heart at a time—through intentional kindness? Wildly waving my hands and hoping you are too. When we practice being where our feet are, opportunities to make a difference *will* surface.

You just might not expect when or how the next one will unfold.

My friend Anjuli recently told me a story of a simple kindness she received one afternoon following an epic meltdown. It started when her neighbor Lindsey stopped by. It was an unplanned visit, but not out of the norm for these friends who often passed the long days of raising littles together. Lindsey's tiny twins joined the fray of Anjuli's three kids. The grown-ups chatted in broken sentences while corralling kiddos and making sure energetic toddlers weren't colliding headfirst into a sharp coffee table corner or each other.

It was your basic Thursday afternoon zoo. And they were happy to be navigating the chaos together. Until it was time for Anjuli's three-year-old son, Samuel, to have a snack.

For Samuel, eating was hard. Not just in the way it's challenging for any picky kid and their parent to agree upon food choices. For Samuel and Anjuli, every bite was a battle. Some might think, *Just lay down the law and make him comply.* But Samuel's failure to gain adequate weight made things more complicated. Every meal, snack, taste, and lick was an agonizing but necessary fight. He *had* to eat. Anjuli never liked having an audience to her son's food issues, but Lindsey was a good enough friend that Anjuli felt okay about continuing their visit while addressing her son's needs. Usually.

On this particular day, Samuel asked for a banana. *Great!* his mama thought. It was one of the few foods the small boy would eat on his own. So with her one-year-old on her hip and one eye on her feisty five-year-old, Anjuli peeled a banana for Samuel. But before the peel was completely removed—as was his banana-eating preference—the banana cracked in half.

Samuel lost it.

The broken banana was like a dagger to his heart. The bloodcurdling screams may have made the mailman think someone was actually being stabbed. Any mama knows that once a wee one with big lungs has crossed over into hysteria, no matter how ridiculous the trigger may be, it's virtually impossible to recover. If you've never been in this situation, *just trust me.*

Still, Anjuli tried to reel Samuel in. She tried to reason with him. She tried to console him. She tried to bribe him and discipline him. As Samuel's tantrum escalated with a front-row audience, Anjuli silently prayed, *Why, God? Why did that have to be the last banana?*

It's hard enough to deal with a kid's meltdown. Especially when it's perhaps the second of the day, or tenth of the week, or you've lost count because you're in the thick of a brutally hard motherhood season. But having someone else witness the unfiltered ugliness, the out-of-controlness of your family and parenting—it makes you want to crawl in a hole and never come out. I know because I've been there.

As Samuel wailed, a blanket of shame wrapped itself around Anjuli. She and Lindsey kept talking. Picking up toys. Sipping coffee. Anjuli kept trying to calm Samuel. If only she could will the clock to rewind, go back in time, and prevent that banana from ever breaking in the first place. If only she could have prevented her heart and pride and happy neighbor playdate from being broken too. But there was no fixing. The darts of insecurity and humiliation kept firing. *What must Lindsey think of me? What kind of mother am I that I can't control my kid, or stop this tantrum, or get him to eat?* Anjuli's internal dialogue spiraled down.

Eventually Lindsey and her little crew left. Anjuli's exhaustion and embarrassment stayed.

The next day Anjuli returned home from running errands and found a bunch of bananas on her doorstep. From Lindsey.

If there's ever been a way to say "I see you. You're not alone" with fruit, this was it! What an incredibly thoughtful gesture of solidarity. I think I would have cried right there.

But what impresses my heart most is that Lindsey had to be present in that hard moment to first see the ache of her friend and then respond in a way that showed love.

Think about it. Lindsey could have easily checked out—mentally or physically. It's not comfortable seeing someone else's child come undone. It's not fun seeing a friend flounder trying to fix the unfixable. Samuel's banana meltdown could have made Lindsey feel awkward enough to go in the other room and scroll Instagram. She could have been annoyed enough to just pick up her littles and leave. But the yellow fruit delivered to Anjuli's doorstep showed that instead Lindsey chose to be exactly where her feet were. She didn't have the power to calm the wailing child. She couldn't rescue her friend from the cycle of food struggles. But Lindsey could pay attention. She could be present with a sympathetic look, a prayer, a helping hand to hold the baby. She could just be there.

And then show up the next day with a bunch of bananas.

This is the beauty of the simple difference. Intentional kindness is an invitation to endless creativity.

But it's not just about the act—it's what it means to one person when connected to one moment.

If Lindsey left bananas on *all* her neighbors' doorsteps, the effect would not have been the same as it was for Anjuli. Maybe someone else would be thankful for, albeit confused by, the surprise. But to one specific mother emerging from her crumb-covered minivan, that bunch of bananas meant everything. It meant she was seen, accepted, and cared for. Those bananas said I'm here for you, cheering for you. You are loved.

Anjuli was so marked by her neighbor's kindness that she decided to encourage others to show up for someone in their life in an unexpected way too. Anjuli issued the Banana Challenge on Instagram.

Commenters got to share creative ideas for how they would lighten someone's load or brighten their day. One winner would receive a fifty-dollar Visa gift card.

"As fun as it was to share my banana story and bless someone with fifty dollars to carry out their own intentional act of kindness," Anjuli recalled, "the real gift came in seeing a flood of ideas for all the ways we can show up in love for our neighbors."

*I'd take my widow neighbor out to dinner.*

*I'd pay for a single mom I know to get her car washed every week.*

*I'd throw my coworker who often seems lonely a birthday party.*

*I'd buy popsicles for the whole neighborhood and let all the kids run in our front yard sprinklers.*

No one else said that they'd gift a bunch of bananas. No one else needed to.

The Banana Challenge did what I hope the simple difference will also do: help open eyes and ready hearts. Help individuals see the potential for their own one-of-a-kind difference making. Help people recognize the beauty, opportunity, and responsibility of *being where our feet are.*

Lindsey was at a neighbor's house for a playdate when her opportunity sparked. Where will you be today? This week? Your next opportunity to make a simple difference in a creative way is probably closer than you think.

Samuel's broken-banana meltdown, Lindsey's banana porch surprise, and Anjuli's Instagram Banana Challenge took place nearly a decade ago. But it's still making an imprint on Anjuli's life. And now on mine. And hopefully on yours. This is the power of small kindness.

The ripple of change widens when we share the good. One small act makes a big impact when we allow kindness received to mark our hearts, reminding us that we are loved, valued, seen. Out of that more healed and whole place, we then grow in our capacity to live eyes wide open to others. We give bananas. We offer standing ovations. We hold doors and put others' needs above our own. We show up on the court for our teammates and on the trail with our family. We are *with*. And our desire and commitment to live the simple difference grows.

Anjuli knows on-your-way, where-your-feet-are kindness is both possible and powerful because she's received it, been changed by it, and passed it on. I hear her story and my heart is marked too. Ripple upon ripple. On and on the circle widens. Waves of change are coming.

### THREE KEYS TO LIVING
*the simple difference*

**Pray it bold.**

*Lord, help me to be where my feet are. Help me to stay mentally, emotionally, and physically present in the moment with the people You put in my path. Make me aware of my tendency to turn my focus inward. Show me how to love one person at a time like You do. Creatively. Intentionally. I'm ready to watch the ripples of kindness widen. May it begin with me. Amen.*

**Live it now.**

- Take stock of all five senses and practice being mindful of your surroundings.
- When you're tempted to mentally turn inward or check out, choose to engage with another right where you are.
- Look for a creative way to remind someone that they are seen and accepted in the middle of their mess.

**Say it loud.**

Today I will be where my feet are.

*nine*

# in it for the long haul

We've talked about how opportunities to impact someone with kindness can crop up unexpectedly in our days. Many interactions with acquaintances or strangers are a one-and-done kind of thing. You stop and pray with the overwhelmed mom in the pediatrician's office. You buy coffee for the person behind you at Starbucks. You find a lost dog and call the number on his collar, or you grab the jar of pasta sauce off the top grocery store shelf for the lady who can't quite reach it. You smile at the server and ask how his day is going even when you'd rather just hurry up and get your order. As brief as these acts of kindness may be, they are still significant.

Beth choosing to brush the old man's hair was significant to him, and it was significant to the airline hostess who witnessed it. May's airport prayer mattered to the woman on the brink of surgery. The kindness of Mary, whose car I hit, mattered to me.

Kindness is personal, every time.

But single-incident kindness is not the only way to live the simple difference. Even more than passing kindness, continual kindness can make a forever mark. Continual kindness means investing in someone's life for the long haul.

Kindness once is a small stone skipped in the large lake of a life. The ripple is visible and meaningful in the moment—but eventually it will fade. Repeated kindness, on the other hand, creates an ongoing impact. Like pebble upon pebble upon pebble ricocheting off the glassy water. The rings of influence widen, the depth of impact deepens. When the stones keep coming, they're sure to create waves of lasting change.

When I think about the impact of perpetual kindness in my life, I think of my friend Esther.

I met Esther my sophomore year of college when she was the new, twentysomething staffer for The Navigators—the campus ministry I was involved in. Navs was a big proponent of discipleship. I didn't really know what it meant to be "discipled," but I longed to grow in my faith and for someone to guide the way.

Esther and I started meeting weekly in my beige cinder block dorm room. We'd sit cross-legged on opposite ends of my periwinkle bedspread for an hour of "discipleship." I guess I expected to learn about the Bible and how to love Jesus more. I thought someone more spiritually mature could keep me accountable in my physical relationship with my boyfriend and my progress with Scripture memory. I was a high achiever and eager to add "good Christian" to my accolades.

But Esther didn't give me a list of spiritual checkboxes. Instead, she taught me what it meant to care for someone's heart. She taught me about the kindness of Jesus by living it.

When Esther asked a question, she leaned in to hear the answer. She was at ease in my awkward silence. She wasn't afraid of the messy parts of my past or how confused I felt about pieces of my present.

Esther just wanted to be with me. She held the brokenness and fears of a straight-A student who may have looked like she had it all together but was actually crumbling under the weight of trying to be enough for everybody—including God. But I didn't have to be enough for Esther. She didn't spend time with college students to get something. She was there to give. With her disarming smile and commitment to meet consistently, Esther made space for me to process past wounds and get to know Jesus, right where I was.

One Thursday afternoon, several months into our meetings, we decided to hang out at Starbucks instead of in my dorm. With mocha Frappuccinos sweating between us, we huddled around a small table along the far wall of windows. Through the haze of time I don't remember the story I told or the problem I was processing, but I do remember how Esther suddenly reached into her bag and pulled out a collapsible keyboard and attached it to her Palm. (Yes, this was long before the days of smartphones and tablets.) As I talked, Esther started typing. I asked what she was doing.

"I usually take notes about our time together later," she explained, "but what you're sharing is really important. I don't want to forget it."

I must have had a strange look on my face because Esther quickly added, "I just want to remember how to pray for you and be able to follow up later on what we've talked about today. Does that make you feel uncomfortable?"

"No. Not uncomfortable." I wiped the tears that emerged without warning. "It makes me feel seen. Loved. Invested in. . . . Like no one ever has."

Esther's thoughtful questions and attentive listening made me feel cared for in a way I had never experienced before. We continued to meet regularly for more than two years. I was sold on the life-changing power of discipleship. But what I came to understand over years of a mentorship-turned-lasting-friendship was that Esther's impact in my life wasn't because of a certain organization or discipleship curriculum (as good as those may be). Esther changed my life because she was one person who showed up over and over to love and serve and see another person.

Her kindness wasn't out of obligation or to fulfill a job description. Her investment in my life went far beyond a part-time position as college ministry staff. She saw me, accepted me, and loved me, right where I was, from right where she was.

Esther let me cry in her arms and bought me cheesy potato soup when I was devastated over a college breakup. On ministry retreats she brought me a baggie of my favorite vanilla chai tea mix and a dose of melatonin in case our loud-sleeping friends kept me awake. When I was on the cusp of a new ministry or career opportunity, she reflected back the ways she saw Jesus working and the gifts He'd given me. She drove the extra distance to talk over cinnamon crunch Panera bagels, again and again and again. She paid for my coffee. When I was getting married, Esther printed one hundred wedding invitations from her home computer and helped me hand-tie one hundred tiny bows. When I was physically and emotionally knotted up with family dysfunction, she crossed half a dozen LA freeways to come rub the tension out of my neck and once again make space for my heart.

These are but a few snapshots of the big impact Esther has made in my life. It's been twenty years since we first sat on my dorm room bed. Over time Esther transitioned from a mentor to a lifelong, soul sister friend.

I'll always be grateful that God used a collegiate ministry to bring Esther into my life. Yet I know her profound influence had nothing to do with titles or programs and everything to do with consistent love and investment.

This is the kind of difference maker we all can be. This is the kind of difference maker Jesus was.

• • •

One of the most remarkable things about Jesus was that He chose to invest His life in close friends. God's Son—full deity who took on full humanity to accomplish the will of the Father and, ya know, save all humankind—chose to spend His short earthly years being a really good friend to some really messy people. Isn't that the best?

Sure, many people had but a single, brief encounter with the Messiah. The woman who reached through the crowd and touched the hem of His robe. The paralyzed man who was lowered through the roof by his friends. The boy who offered his meager lunch. The blind man who received sight for the very first time through a mixture of spit and dirt and Jesus's miracle touch. Yes, Jesus made a life-changing impact in the lives of these people through a single moment or meeting.

But even more, think about the disciples. Think about the inner circle of men and women with whom Jesus shared life. The ones He showed up for time and time again. The ones He saw at their worst and loved anyway. The continual kindness of their friend Jesus made all the difference.

The ripple of His influence in their lives created waves of lasting change.

Take Peter, for example. Oh, Peter. God bless him. He was passionate and impulsive. He reacted before he paused to think. He interrupted and contradicted often. He trusted Jesus and then let fear overtake him. He swore his loyalty to Jesus and then three times betrayed Him. Suffice it to say, Peter wasn't a perfect friend. And yet Jesus loved him again and again. Jesus showed up on the shore and in the storm. He predicted Peter's duplicity and still welcomed him with open arms.

Jesus broke bread. Washed feet. Poured out His heart. Not once or twice but relentlessly to give His friends all He had.

He did this for two sisters too. He showed up for Mary and Martha when things were good and when the unthinkable happened. They shared meals and long conversations. Can you think of a better picture of life-together friendship?

What really gives credit to the authenticity and impact of their friendship is the fact that Martha wasn't afraid to express her frustration and ask Jesus a hard question. The story unfolds in Luke 10. Jesus and the disciples come to the village of Bethany and stay in the home of two sisters, Martha and Mary. While Martha gets to work preparing food and drinks for her houseful of guests, Mary sits with Jesus and hangs on His every word.

Martha can't handle the inequity, and she doesn't keep quiet about it. "Lord, don't you care that my sister has left me to do the work by myself? Tell her to help me!"

Does that not sound like the voice of a friend close enough to be like a sister? Martha calls Him Lord out of respect, but her words reveal that Jesus was a familiar guest. If this were the first time they had met, surely Martha would have maintained a more formal tone, shown more restraint, stifled the exasperation she felt toward her unhelpful sister and the demands of hosting. But good friends don't need to suppress their feelings or use a filter. They say it like it is. And that's exactly what busy, distracted, irritated Martha did. (I kind of love her for it.)

Jesus's response confirms the nature of their friendship. "'Martha, Martha,' the Lord answered, 'you are worried and upset about many things, but few things are needed—or indeed only one. Mary has chosen what is better, and it will not be taken away from her.'"[1]

Jesus wasn't afraid to answer Martha with the truth she probably didn't want to hear. Yet the disarming gentleness of a friend who has her best interest at heart lessens the sting of a painful reality check.

*Martha, Martha.* He uses her name twice. He knows her. He knows how she is wired, how she gets so tightly wound and loses sight of what's truly important. He probably also knows all about their family dynamics and any underlying tension between the sisters. Jesus doesn't rebuke Martha's brutal honesty like an elite leader or stranger casting judgment. He responds like a friend. Calling her out and up and loving her, right where she is.

• • •

The next time we see these two sisters encounter Jesus, Martha is grieving something far more serious than unevenly divided chores. Her brother, Lazarus, has died. Jesus knew Lazarus was sick because "the sisters sent word to Jesus, 'Lord, the one you love is sick.'" When He heard the news, Jesus responded, "This sickness will not end in death. No, it is for God's glory so that God's Son may be glorified through it." But then Jesus delayed going to His friend's aid, which made no sense to the disciples because they knew Jesus loved this trio of siblings.

If He loved them, why wouldn't He rush to help?

Eventually Jesus does travel back to Bethany. When Martha gets word that Jesus is on His way, she goes out to meet Him. But Mary stays home. The first words out of Martha's mouth sound a little different than the last we heard from her. "Lord, if you had been here, my brother would not have died. But I know that even now God will give you whatever you ask."

She laments but she trusts. She knows Jesus is not only her friend but also her Messiah. She knows He is both faithful and able, but she can't ignore the reality of death and the pang of her grief.

Martha returns to the house where Mary is with the mourners who have come to offer her comfort. She tells her sister that Jesus is asking for her. Hearing this, Mary quickly goes to Jesus. But when she sees

Him, her response isn't as composed as her sister's. She falls to His feet and weeps. "Lord, if you had been here, my brother would not have died."

And this is the part of the story that I'll never get over. As Jesus sees Mary weeping and others mourning, He is "deeply moved in spirit and troubled." Then Jesus weeps too.[2]

He enters the sorrow and suffering of His friends. Despite the fact that Jesus had already foretold Lazarus's resurrection to both Martha and the disciples, Lazarus was dead. The weight of death is never light.

So in the heaviness, Jesus wept.

Consider how Jesus *could* have responded. He could have patted Mary on the head and told her that her tears were for nothing because He was about to bring Lazarus back to life. He could have scolded her for not trusting Him more. He could have given a "just wait and see" sermon about the power of God. But this moment wasn't about what Jesus knew was to come; it was about how His friends grieved in the present. And Jesus was present for it.

I have known no deeper kindness in my own life than a friend sitting beside me and bearing witness to my grief. Not minimizing my loss. Not trying to alleviate the uncomfortable reality of my sobbing. Not putting an inadequate Band-Aid on my pain with a Bible verse or "it could be worse" platitude. No fixing or judging or explaining. Just the simple, extravagant kindness of being with. Entering in.

This posture of coming alongside another with compassion and taking on their burden as our own is surely what the apostle Paul had in mind when he instructed believers to "Rejoice with those who rejoice; mourn with those who mourn."[3]

If I know how it felt when my friend Esther held me as I cried ugly tears over the death of a relationship, how it felt when friends and coworkers showed up to my father's funeral, then I can only imagine the deep love and comfort Mary and Martha felt when their friend, their Lord Jesus, wept alongside them.

This is the kindness of Christ.

His tearstained face also spoke volumes to those who witnessed. "Then the Jews said, 'See how he loved him!'"[4]

Perhaps this observation was a foreshadowing of one of Jesus's final encouragements to His closest friends: "A new command I give you: Love one another. As I have loved you, so you must love one another. By this everyone will know that you are my disciples, if you love one another."[5]

The way Jesus grieved with His friends was like saying, *Look! The way you love one another, how you help and weep and do life together, will be your greatest testimony to who I am.*

At this point in the story, Jesus follows Mary and Martha, along with those who had gathered, to Lazarus's tomb. He tells them to roll away the stone. In typical Martha fashion, she pipes up with practicality. "But, Lord, by this time there is a bad odor, for he has been there four days."[6] Oh, Martha. Still fighting that urge to believe she knows best.

Jesus replies, "Did I not tell you that if you believe, you will see the glory of God?"

At that, the stone is removed from the cave entrance and Jesus calls in a loud voice, "Lazarus, come out!"[7]

The dead man, friend, and brother walks out!

Revel in this miracle. Then camp out on this thought: Jesus went to extraordinary lengths to meet Mary and Martha in their grief and raise Lazarus from the dead because *He knew them* and He loved them.

The kindness of a long-haul friend is the kindness of God. This is who Jesus was and who He invites us to be.

Jesus did not reserve His impact for large crowds and synagogue courtyards. He came to change the world but knew mass influence was not the only way to do it. The size of the audience didn't matter. Jesus cared about the one and the few.

In today's culture, bigger often looks better. We applaud those with bestselling books, popular podcasts, and massive social media reach. We are impressed when superstar sports heroes, Grammy Award winners, and Hollywood celebrities leverage their wealth and fame to help the masses. But we'd be wrong to believe that big name influencers are the only ones who can make a meaningful difference. We'd be remiss to delegate the biggest impact to church pulpits or conference stages or sold-out arenas.

Sometimes the greatest impact we can make is showing up for a friend, again and again. Sometimes the greatest difference we can make is caring for one person's heart for the long haul.

One parent in your playgroup. One college student at your church. One teenager in your home. One neighbor on your street from another part of the world. One friend who sometimes gets bossy and mouthy and distracted.

Let's change the world like Jesus did—by simply being there. Leaning in to listen. Opening our arms to hold. Weeping together. As often and as long as it takes.

## THREE KEYS TO LIVING
*the simple difference*

**Pray it bold.**

*Jesus, thank You for showing what it means to be a friend who loves consistently. Help me to really understand how investing in one or two relationships matters just as much as (or maybe more than) influencing the masses. Show me one person I can care for today and tomorrow and continually like You do. Amen.*

**Live it now.**

- Ask a friend how they're doing and lean in to really listen to the answer.
- Consider who you could intentionally care for and invest in. Initiate a time to get together with that person.
- Show up for a friend who is struggling or grieving. Don't try to fix their pain. Just be with.

**Say it loud.**

Consistent kindness leads to big influence.

*ten*

# unexpected teachers

As a mom of three, I feel an added responsibility not only to live a life of kindness for myself but to teach my kids to be kind humans. I know this isn't new to me or new to parenthood. Probably since the beginning of time, mothers and fathers have been telling their children to be kind, show respect, mind their manners. We tell our kids to follow the golden rule—treat others the way you would want to be treated. (Or maybe you're like me and rather than "telling," you also catch yourself lecture-yelling in an awful tone about how they need to speak kindly. Yikes. I've still got lots of learning to do.)

While raising up our kids to be caring, courteous, and responsible citizens isn't a new parental obligation, it feels even harder in today's digital age. Raising a device-in-hand generation makes the task of training kids to truly see others even more challenging than in simpler times when society was less me-centered, with fewer perpetual distractions. I imagine all the parents, teachers, and coaches are nodding in solidarity.

Sometimes I look at today's youth and I feel a little discouraged about their willingness and ability to be simple difference world changers. Is the next generation able to look up? Are they willing to see beyond their own comfort and needs and glowing screen?

I've almost gotten mowed over by a teen on a speeding skateboard who was texting instead of paying attention. I've smiled and said hello to a pair of junior highers walking home from school, only to be met with a blank stare or ignored altogether. Some of this could be attributed to a lack of spatial awareness or shyness. But I think it's more about being self-focused.

Loving others requires selflessness. Kindness requires awareness. Both of these qualities seem to be in short supply. When my family goes grocery shopping, I'm constantly telling my kids to be alert. It's their nature to wander in the middle of the frozen food aisle, oblivious to other shoppers. They need continual reminders to be considerate of the people around them. At Costco we see kids pushing their way to the front of a crowded sample line. Small hands dart in to snatch flimsy paper cups filled with popcorn or chocolate, totally unaware of (or unconcerned about) all the people they cut in front of.

But the issues with today's youth culture extend far beyond poor manners. There's not just a lack of intentional kindness, there's also an accepted cycle of active harassment. A recent national survey confirmed what so many tragic news stories have suggested: bullying among kids and teens—both in person and online—is steadily on the rise.[1] Building yourself up at the cost of tearing others down has become grossly normal. I've seen a friend's daughter bullied on Instagram. Degrading lies spewed in captions aimed at getting likes and comments.

Kindness cannot coexist with these types of self-serving, others-abusing behaviors. We have to do better.

This is just a narrow glimpse at the darker side of what's happening among today's youth. I share it because it burdens me as a parent and a citizen of our world. In order to do better we have to be aware of where we're falling short. Yet for all the adolescent eyeballs glued to phones and lack of social skills, for all the ways tablets and smartphones have become insufficient babysitters for today's children, despite how social media has ratcheted up cyberbullying and anxiety and decreased our collective ability to engage in authentic face-to-face interaction—there is hope.

These disheartening examples are not the whole story.

Not only is there hope for the kids growing up in our homes and neighborhoods, there are children who are already beautiful and as-tounding examples of simple difference makers. We can learn from them every day. We've just got to pay attention.

I had this kind of learning moment a few years ago when I overheard a conversation on a school playground. Walking my kindergartener to class, we took a shortcut across the first-grade blacktop. Children were busy playing hopscotch and four square, absorbed in their own asphalt worlds. Suddenly a little girl bolted from a nearby classroom and ran right in front of us toward another girl, shouting, "There's a new student! We have a new student!"

Her friend lunged toward her with a skip and a hop. Eyes wide with delight, she shouted back, "A new student? In our class?"

The first friend nodded yes and both girls broke into glorious grins and galloped toward the brick building to welcome their new friend. Yes, it was beautifully obvious that they had already decided this new student would be their *friend*. Without knowing the student's race or gender, whether they packed a lunch or would buy in the cafeteria, without knowing the color of their hair or if they wore glasses, before knowing if this student liked soccer or handball or My Little Pony, they wanted this student to be their friend. These girls didn't need to know if the new student would get picked up by their dad or go to daycare, whether they were good at reading or math or needed extra help with everything . . . without knowing anything other than the promise of their presence, the two first graders unconditionally accepted their peer.

I wish I could have followed the girls inside that classroom to witness the moment that new student received their warm welcome. Would the gift of instant friends ease the knot in their stomach? Would the bright smiles of those eager to meet them turn nervous fidgeting into a shared grin? I think it's safe to say that being enthusiastically accepted made a big difference in the new student's day—maybe it even impacted their whole week, year, or school career.

I can't help but wonder what life would be like if we all embraced someone new and unknown with the same excitement as those wide-eyed and tenderhearted six-year-olds. As adults we like to wait and size people up. We're tentative to open our hearts or minds or lives to others before going through a thorough checklist. An intentional or subconscious "Are you worthy of my attention and affection?" evaluation, if you will.

We wait to see how many boxes the new person will tick that align with our preferences:

- ☐ Personality
- ☐ Education
- ☐ Hobbies
- ☐ Cultural expressions
- ☐ Political or religious views
- ☐ Career path

☐ Family makeup and dynamics

☐ Financial status

☐ Culinary likes, dislikes, and skills

☐ Do they have Disneyland hookups or a retail discount I could take advantage of?

We withhold our friendship until we know whether we will get along or if they always wear that much perfume. Have you ever been guilty of judging someone by a first impression? Maybe even assigning value based on their surface appearance? Gulp. I have. And if you're honest, I'm guessing you're not exempt either.

It's not that every person needs to be a BFF, trusted confidant, or an intimate part of our lives. But every person does deserve to be respected and treated with kindness. So rather than leading with subtle scrutiny and secret judgment, what if we made acceptance our default? What would happen if we automatically saw the new guy at work or woman behind us at church, the family that just moved in next door or the parent standing alone on the soccer sidelines as a welcomed new friend? What would happen if we treated every "new kid" (young or old) as wanted, welcomed, delighted in?

Sit with that for a minute.

After dropping Jude off, I walked back across the blacktop, through the freshly cut grass, and out the rear school gate with a smile stretched across my face. Two six-year-olds were simple difference makers—not only to the new students they welcomed but to me. A thirtysomething woman who merely overheard their kindness was impacted. And now the ripple extends to you as I share their story. The students at Cullen Elementary School were there to learn, yet able to teach so much.

May the learning continue with us.

• • •

Despite my opening complaints about how my sons are often oblivious to other grocery store shoppers (someone please tell me they will eventually grow in spatial awareness and consideration of strangers), there are times when my kids can be remarkably perceptive to the feelings and needs of those around them.

The other day at Noah's soccer game, Elias and Jude asked if they could go hang out at the nearby playground. They are old enough to be watched at a distance, so I gave them permission. At halftime I walked over, expecting to find Jude swinging from the monkey bars and Elias hunting for worms. Instead I discovered my sons sweetly rolling a ball down the slide and into the arms of a waiting toddler. Every time the little boy caught the ball he squealed with joy. I watched the scene on repeat. Over and over again my big kids retrieved the orange ball and released it down the slide for the delight of their little friend.

Eventually Jude looked up and saw my pleased yet quizzical expression.

"He looked sad and didn't have anyone to play with, so we wanted to make him happy," my boy said.

"That's great, buddy," I called.

Turning to go back to the soccer game, I noticed a mom sitting on a concrete bench, nursing a baby. She caught my eye and nodded toward the slide with a tired, grateful smile. Oh, I remember those baby-nursing, toddler-chasing days so well.

My kids thought they were just being kind to a fussy toddler with rosy cheeks and chubby fingers. But the ripple of their willingness to notice the person in front of them widened to touch the heart of his weary mom, and then to me. Their simple awareness and playful response to someone in need makes me want to see others around me too.

While some kids can be totally oblivious to those around them—isn't that true of us all at times?—other children have a special ability to sense the needs and feelings of others. My friend Lisa Leonard's son David is that kind of kid. David has a rare genetic condition called Cornelia de Lange syndrome, which makes him unable to speak and small in stature. He has only two fingers on one hand, along with a host of other cognitive and medical issues. Yet David has a beautiful way of seeing people.

Lisa shares one example of the simple difference David has made in her book *Brave Love*.[2] She writes,

---

We arrived at church a few minutes early. David held my hand as he slowly climbed the front steps of the church, one at a time. Once inside, he pulled away from me. He wanted to explore the sanctuary before the service began.

David was nonverbal, but we were learning that he still had much to say. He communicated by taking our hands and leading us to what he wanted. He spoke through gestures, physical touch, and heart connection. I followed him around the sanctuary as he slid his hand over the smooth wood of the church pews, weaving in and out of the narrow spaces. Then he crossed the aisle and made his way over to a woman sitting by herself. She looked to be in her late thirties, and she had a kind face and a gentle presence.

We had never met this woman, but that didn't stop David from approaching her. He was rarely shy and seemed to have a knack for approaching people who were warm and loving. As he got closer, the woman looked up and smiled at him. Once beside her, David turned around and backed up to her—his way of asking to be held.

"He wants to sit on your lap," I explained. "He can sit next to you if you prefer."

159

"No," she said. "I'd love to hold him." She carefully lifted him onto her lap. He tenderly wrapped his arm around her neck and laid his head against her shoulder.

"Is this okay?" I asked, anxious to be considerate of her. "Would you like me to move him?" She looked up at me with tears in her eyes.

"My mom was diagnosed with cancer a couple days ago," she said in a quiet voice. "I just needed a hug so badly. He knew exactly what I needed."

I knelt beside them and touched her knee softly as she and David embraced. It was a holy moment of connection that soothed her hurting heart. In that moment, David, who had a disability and was nonverbal, poured out love to a stranger, offering her comfort and connection.

———

Kindness and compassion come in all shapes and so many unexpected ways. David may not have the ability to run across a blacktop to welcome a new student, or the strength to hold a door for someone, or the voice to offer a kind word, but boy, does he make a big impact by offering the love and kindness of his presence. David sees people. He listens and speaks through his heart.

As I think about this moment and the impact it had on the woman sitting alone in church with her unspoken grief, I recognize that David isn't the only one who made a simple difference. David's mom, Lisa, also showed a willingness to live eyes wide open to the people in front of her—including her son.

I think about how many times I've arrived at church exhausted from the effort of getting myself and little people presentably dressed without toothpaste or cereal on our shirts, out the door, buckled in the car, into a parking space (without hitting another car), and finally through the church door. Being on time (let alone early) would feel like a Sunday morning miracle. I can picture myself in Lisa's shoes and how my own young sons would like to explore the sanctuary, see all the people, touch all the things. It would be easier for me to corral them into our chosen seats than let them explore. My default would be to side with my own comfort rather than their desire to stretch their legs and roam the aisles. I love that Lisa chose what was better for her son over what was easier for herself.

Then I think about the moment David approached the woman and sat on her lap. Lisa could have let her worry over whether David was intruding override her willingness to engage with a stranger. She could have been more concerned with appearance than with connection.

Part of learning from our kids is learning to trust them and their unique gifts. Despite her own anxiety, Lisa stayed in the moment. She didn't assume David was being an imposition or inconvenience. She asked a question to make sure they were being respectful, but Lisa didn't run, hide, or pull away—even when that would have been the more comfortable thing to do. Because Lisa was willing to follow her son's lead and enter into someone's space, she had the privilege of entering into their story too.

David wasn't afraid of awkwardness. He was intent on connecting with someone's heart.

How much we have to learn from those younger and seemingly less able than ourselves. The weakest among us may be the strongest in compassion—and that is true strength indeed.

• • •

I recently read another story of a remarkable compassion-in-action kid and her supportive mom. Eight-year-old Ryleigh Livengood and her mom, Tiffany, were getting ready to leave their local Walmart when Ryleigh noticed that there were shopping carts strewn all over the parking lot and only one worker trying to collect them all. Ryleigh asked her mom if they could help.

"That's what we're supposed to do. We're supposed to be kind," she told her mom. Ryleigh didn't put away just one cart. Or two carts. For thirty minutes the mother-daughter duo collected row after row of carts from all over the large parking lot and pushed them to CJ Hart, a Walmart employee. When Ryleigh had pushed the last cart to CJ, she gave him a high five and they parted ways.

The next time the mom and daughter went to Walmart, Ryleigh immediately saw a rogue cart up on a curb and pushed it into the store, where she spotted her new friend CJ hard at work again.

"A little while later, while browsing toys, CJ walks up and hands Ryleigh a thank-you card with $20. After reading the card, Ryleigh went around the aisle to hug him," Tiffany shared on social media.

Inside the card CJ wrote a message that said, "Your hard work meant a lot to me. I don't know you, but you're an angel."

CJ was moved by a little girl who went out of her way for the sake of helping another person. The young man then chose to show his appreciation, and Ryleigh was touched by his kindness in return.

Her mom wrote, "Ryleigh put the card on her dresser so it would remind her to always be kind."[3]

Do you see how kindness begets kindness? One ripple triggers another.

I look at this story with both heart-warmed wonder and real-life practicality, and I see *three* amazing simple difference makers. Ryleigh, of course. CJ, absolutely. But Mama Tiffany too! I don't know about you, but when I'm done shopping at Walmart, especially if I have a child in tow, I am *done*. I've usually got a fluorescent-light-induced headache, I'm irritated by the crowds and long wait, and I forgot my reusable bags along with the list I left at home so now I have ten things I don't need and forgot the three things I really do. So as I load my trunk, I'm not really in the stop-and-clean-up-the-mess-of-other-lazy-shoppers kinda mood. (If you have no idea what I'm talking about then just pray for me and move along.) But if you *know* this feeling, then you know how extraordinary it is that Tiffany said *yes* to delaying her Walmart departure!

She might have had ice cream melting in her car or lunch meat getting questionably warm. She might have had more errands to run or dinner to get in the oven or a part-time job to get home to. We don't have to know her exact circumstances to know that this mom was willing to postpone whatever was next on her agenda for the sake of empowering her daughter to help another.

I want to be like Tiffany and Ryleigh and CJ. I want to be like Lisa and David. I want to be like my boys on the playground and the schoolgirls running to welcome a new student. I hope you do too.

Today let's choose to help others as we go on our way.

Let's see the people around us. Let's use our time and presence, our joy and enthusiasm (despite our own inconvenience or irritation) to let others know that their feelings and needs and workloads matter.

I have a lot to teach my three sons as they grow up. But I'm convinced now more than ever that children can be our greatest unexpected teachers. It's time we lean in and learn.

### THREE KEYS TO LIVING
## *the simple difference*

**Pray it bold.**

*God, like a teenager glued to a cell phone, I confess it's easy for me to live eyes down, consumed with myself. Help me to pursue connection over my own agenda. Show me how to choose kindness over my own comfort. Make me teachable and moldable and ready to jump up and down in excitement and jump in to help another—just like a child. Amen.*

**Live it now.**

- Make acceptance your default. The next time you encounter someone new to your neighborhood, workplace, or group, welcome them with open arms.
- Look for the person who needs a friend—on the playground, in the church pew—and let compassion move you.
- Choose one small way to help someone without being asked. Return a shopping cart, pick up trash, hold the door, go last.

**Say it loud.**

The simple gift of my presence and acceptance can make a difference.

*eleven*

# giving your not-enough

The simple difference is all about giving something of ourselves for the sake of someone else. Giving our time, our words, our prayers, our awkwardness, our humility. A helping hand, a friendly smile, a twenty-dollar bill. But let's talk about what we do when we feel like we don't have anything to give. Or like what we've got isn't possibly enough to accomplish anything. I've felt it. I'm sure you have too.

We're aware of so many needs around us. Good, valid, worthy, desperate needs. We want to make a difference in our community—help the youth, the elderly, the marginalized, the forgotten. But between our own pressing needs and responsibilities, we don't have any margin to volunteer our time or get involved with a cause. We know people who are suffering from a natural disaster, an extended season of unemployment, or a devastating diagnosis; financial support could offer some relief, but our own budgets are already squeezed. We want to be good people, help a loved one or a neighbor, but we don't seem to have the right skills or answers or resources . . . so we do nothing.

Or I guess I should speak for myself. Many times I have seen opportunities to help—even felt that familiar Holy Spirit nudge—and yet I didn't respond. Why?

The answer has much less to do with my bank account balance or empty spots on my calendar and everything to do with the fact that part of me still doubts that what I have to offer is enough to really make a difference. Is that totally awful to admit? I told you I'm no kindness poster child. After writing all of these words, I can still wrestle with trusting that my small, barely perceptible acts of kindness can actually impact the world.

The problems feel paralyzing. Homelessness. Racism. Refugees. Hunger. Human trafficking. To name but a few of the many widespread, deep-rooted, pervasive, complex issues facing our world. Or even take it down a notch (or fifty) to a much smaller scale. Maybe like me, you have a friend or family member who just keeps getting knocked down. Life keeps handing them the short end of the stick. Their layers of suffering are deep. You want to fix it all, redeem all the broken pieces, give them a redo—but you can't. You can't solve the totality of their problems, so you default to a nonresponse.

We each look at our one little life, and it seems painfully obvious that we're not powerful enough, knowledgeable enough, affluent enough, or equipped enough to understand the countless facets and nuances of these problems, let alone do anything to change them. The temptation then is to numb over and disconnect.

Or maybe you *do* understand because you've been living through it yourself, but you still don't have the power or privilege to overturn a broken system or rescue those who are flailing alongside you.

For many of us—for me and I believe for you too—our action paralysis isn't a reflection of our lack of care, but a lack of faith to believe that our care can make a difference.

So if doubt, cynicism, or uncertainty about the legitimacy of simple difference living is still lingering in the periphery of your mind (or it's like a flashing neon sign front and center), you are not alone. You do not have to hide your doubts here. This is the place to name the barriers that hold us back and hold our questions up to the light of God's Word.

Let me tell you this, friend: one of my most favorite things about the Lord is that He is not afraid of, bothered by, or critical of our feelings.

There isn't one question or emotion that God can't handle. You can scream and shout. Cry and doubt. You won't be too much for Him. If your faith is wavering and your feet are wandering and you need assurance that God is real and near and He cares, ask Him. He won't turn His back or tune you out. Like I said at the get-go of this book, question-asking is often the beginning of seeing. And seeing is the beginning of believing.

This is important for us to grasp, because if you cannot be honest with God, you will not trust Him. If you don't know this side of God's character, hang out in the Psalms. Many were written by David, who was a big-time question asker and emotion sharer. David saw God's faithfulness over and over, yet again and again he needed to be reminded of it. In Psalm 31 David expresses his distress, his grief, his affliction—life is not going well for him. David's honesty before God leads him to this resolve: "But I trust in you, LORD; I say, 'You are my God.' The course of my life is in your power."[1] In Psalm 103 David coaches his own heart, saying, "Let all that I am praise the LORD; may I never forget the good things he does for me."[2] And then he goes on to recite what those good things are.

Rehearsing the truth of who God is and recalling His faithfulness in our lives is crucial to remembering that He will do it again. Faith is living like we know He will continue to be faithful.

Why is believing so hard?

I don't know about you, but I want things to make sense. The simple difference doesn't always fit that description. It's a backward, upside-down economy. How does a little bit turn into a lot? How can one tiny pebble create a wave of change? Sounds too good to be true.

Kind of like the gospel.

The life of one paid for the sins of all.

In God's economy grace multiplies. Beauty comes from ashes. The last will be first. Manna rains from heaven. Life springs from a womb long barren. The lesson repeats itself all throughout Scripture. Take what you know and let God flip it around.

• • •

On our simple difference journey, we must remember that we can't see the whole picture. But God can.

I try to understand my limited point of view by imagining it like this: I'm standing alone at the base of a large mountain. The mountain is a massive need, issue, or problem. I can't see any way through, over, or around it. The mountain is casting a large shadow over me. I feel overwhelmed and dwarfed by the magnitude of it. All I have is a small shovel, weak arms, and a tiny window of time. Trying to meet the need, address the issue, or fix the problem feels like attempting to move the entire mountain by myself, one shovelful at a time. Impossible. Why even try? My efforts would be futile, right? Better to save my shovel, conserve my energy, spend my time on something more manageable. Better to ignore the mountain altogether. Better to work toward a goal that's actually achievable. It's just good logic, don't you think? Common sense wins.

But what if what seems so obvious and clear-cut from where I'm standing doesn't reflect the whole picture from a different vantage point? What if I'm not actually alone?

Around the next bend, outside of the shadow, someone else is standing with a shovel. And beyond his line of sight there's another person. And another after her. In fact, the whole mountain is surrounded by shovel wielders. Each person feels alone, wondering if they have what it takes to make a small dent, let alone a big change. But no one is truly alone. We may each be poised to tackle a different nook or cranny, but we encircle the Goliath together.

Not only that, but in the clouds that hug each peak, in the wind that rustles through the towering trees, in the heart of each man and woman staggered around the base of this mountain, is the staggering power and presence of God.

What we can't see or fully understand is clear from God's view: the mountain won't move by our feeble strength and inadequate tools, but it can be moved by His power at work in us. It's like Ephesians 3:20 says, "Now all glory to God, who is able, through his mighty power at work within us, to accomplish infinitely more than we might ask or think" (NLT).

His power. Through us.

But we've gotta have faith. It's crucial to the work God wants to do in and through us.

In Matthew 17 we find a distressed father who is desperately seeking healing for his son who is possessed by a demon. Jesus's disciples try to heal him, but they cannot. Jesus doesn't hide His frustration. "'What a generation! No sense of God! No focus to your lives! How many times do I have to go over these things? How much longer do I have to put up with this? Bring the boy here.' He ordered the afflicting demon out—and it was out, gone. From that moment on the boy was well."[3]

Now, if I'm honest, I'm a little taken aback by Jesus's response. I mean, the disciples are just human. Jesus, on the other hand, is fully

169

God in human form. So how can He expect ordinary men to accomplish the impossible like He can?

Yet the disciples don't seem as concerned with Jesus's exasperated rebuke. They just want to know why they couldn't drive out this demon. They had healed people before. What gives? "'Because you're not yet taking *God* seriously,' said Jesus. 'The simple truth is that if you had a mere kernel of faith, a poppy seed, say, you would tell this mountain, "Move!" and it would move. There is nothing you wouldn't be able to tackle.'"[4] Another translation says it this way: "Truly I tell you, if you have faith as small as a mustard seed, you can say to this mountain, 'Move from here to there,' and it will move. Nothing will be impossible for you."

*"Nothing will be impossible for you."* Let that wash over you.

The disciples saw the problem. God sees the possibility.

I hear the echo of Jesus's words in the closing of Paul's letter to the Ephesians. "I pray that out of his glorious riches he may **strengthen** you with **power** through his Spirit in your inner being, so that Christ may dwell in your hearts through **faith**."[5] Reread those words in bold. Ask God right in this moment to show you connections between His strength and power and your faith.

Now keep listening. "And I pray that you, being rooted and established in love, may have power, together with all the Lord's holy people, to grasp how wide and long and high and deep is the love of Christ, and to know this love that surpasses knowledge—that you may be filled to the measure of all the fullness of God."[6] Throughout this book our conversation about living the simple difference has continually pointed back to loving others because God first loved us. I'll be the clang of an annoying cymbal if that's what it takes to make someone reading hear—*really hear*—that all of this always points back to God's love.

Want to change the world? Or just make your one small life count? Ask God for the power to grasp the width and length and depth of His love for you.

The end of Paul's letter could be our simple difference motto: "Now to him who is able to do *immeasurably more* than all we ask or imagine, **according to his power that is at work within us."**[7]

Immeasurably more.

Think back to that image of standing in the mountain's shadow. What a single person can do with a small shovel, God can do immeasurably more.

Take to heart the way The Message translates this verse: "God can do anything, you know—far more than you could ever imagine or guess or request in your wildest dreams! He does it not by pushing us around but by working within us, his Spirit deeply and gently within us."

This must be what Jesus meant when He said, "Nothing will be impossible for you." Nothing is impossible for you, not because you try hard or care deeply or are smart, strong, talented, influential, or admired. Nothing is impossible when the power of God's Spirit is working within you!

● ● ●

To live the simple difference, we have to exchange the way we see our not-enough for the way God sees it.

God doesn't expect us to give something we don't have. He invites us to give what we *do* have.

Perhaps the most iconic example of this is the boy who gave his five loaves of bread and two fish. If you're not familiar with the story, it's found in all four of the Gospels—a fact alone that points to its significance in Scripture and the ministry of Jesus. Here's the super-quick rundown. A huge crowd—five thousand men, plus women and children—has been following Jesus and His disciples, eager to see Him heal the sick. They are in a remote location. It's getting late, which is problematic because there isn't enough food to feed the crowd and no easy place to get some. Plus, as Philip points out in the John 6 account, "It would take more than half a year's wages to buy enough bread for each one to have a bite!"

Then Andrew, another disciple, pipes up, "Here is a boy with five small barley loaves and two small fish, but how far will they go among so many?" In essence he's saying, look at what we have—it's something, but it's not enough. Have you ever done this? You're aware of a huge problem or predicament, you want to do something to help, but the resources available to you fall painfully short. It's a why-bother, shackled-by-the-impossible moment.

Or perhaps you read this story and rather than wanting to help, your default response is *everyone for themselves!* Why was it up to Jesus and the disciples to feed all these people anyway? Every adult should exercise personal responsibility. Plan ahead or suffer the consequences, right? I know some highly left-brain people who would see this as the clear solution and wouldn't hesitate to disperse the crowd in an orderly fashion to go acquire their own sustenance. If that's you, there's a lesson for you here too.

We don't know if the boy who gave up his meager meal did so willingly or begrudgingly. What we do know is that Jesus transformed what was not enough into more than enough.

Jesus then took the loaves, gave thanks, and distributed to those who were seated as much as they wanted. He did the same with the fish. When they had all had enough to eat, he said to his disciples, "Gather the pieces that are left over. Let nothing be wasted." So they gathered them and filled twelve baskets with the pieces of the five barley loaves left over by those who had eaten.[8]

Scripture doesn't tell us if the boy held out hope that his little lunch would help or if it felt like an empty gesture toward a lost cause. But here's the thing: how we feel or what we think about the resources we have to give doesn't dictate or limit God's power to use them. Did you catch that? It wasn't up to the boy what became of his food. It was up to him to be aware of the needs around him, assess the resources available to him, and respond to the opportunity to make a difference.

The boy was willing. He gave all he had. That was all that God asked.

This startling miracle of multiplication was fueled by God's power! Only He could take a total lack and turn it into total satisfaction. But the spark that started the blaze of provision was one small act of obedience.

This story gives me so much hope.

Time and time again I'm faced with what I perceive as my own inadequacy and lack. What I have to give rarely feels enough for what is needed. A friend needs help moving, but I don't have a truck. Someone needs a babysitter, but I'm buried with work. A family can't pay rent, but what I have to give can hardly make a dent. In times like these we need to remember that God's power fills in the gap.

We have the delightful opportunity to show up, give freely, and put the responsibility of the outcome squarely where it belongs—in God's sovereign hands.

• • •

The story of those five small barley loaves and two fish came to mind recently when I heard about a friend in need.

This happened in the thick of COVID-19 first hitting the US hard. As shelter-in-place restrictions came into effect, along with the widespread shutdown of businesses and services, I was naturally concerned about how the pandemic was impacting my friends. Amid mass layoffs and companies on the brink of bankruptcy, so many individuals and families were facing challenging, if not devastating, circumstances.

One evening I checked in with my friend Elise to see how her family of eight was doing. She and her husband both did a range of jobs as independent contractors. Jason worked in construction and as a handyman, and Elise was a makeup artist and speaker. All their streams of income were squashed with the swift and strict shutdown of their Texas town.

"Are you guys okay?" I asked.

Over Voxer messages and across thousands of miles, Elise shared the messy answer to my question. Countless jobs had been scrapped. Work orders canceled. Clients lost. Her family was more than okay in the sense that they were home, together, and trusting boldly in their Provider. God had always been faithful. He had a history of teaching Elise how to be content in times of plenty and times of want. In another sense, Elise didn't know how they were going to buy groceries to feed their six children.

I sat on my couch folding laundry, reading Elise's messages. The gravity of her situation sank into my heart as tears streamed down my cheeks. Sadly, Elise's circumstances were not unique. That week my inbox and social media feed had been flooded with opportunities to help meet immediate, desperate needs of friends and strangers.

In my dimly lit living room, I felt much like that boy must have, holding his loaves and fish, looking out at the crowd of thousands. I wished Los Angeles and Houston weren't so far apart. I'd drive right over to Elise's house if I could and deliver dinner for the night and groceries for the week. Part of me wished we hadn't already helped someone else in need so that I would have more to now give my friend.

I searched for pairs of socks in the mismatched pile and prayed. I asked my God to help my friend—His beloved daughter. I asked Him to transform her not-enough into miraculous abundance, just like those twelve baskets full of leftover bread. In the midst of that prayer, I wrestled my strong desire to help with the reality of my own limitations. I said amen and opened my Venmo app. I was hoping to find a surplus of forgotten dollars stored there from book sales at speaking events earlier that spring. But sure enough, that money had already been transferred or spent or given away. All but eleven dollars.

When you hear that one of your dearest friends doesn't know where her next meal is going to come from, eleven dollars seems laughable. Yet this is exactly what God asked me to give.

*Give what you have. All of your little is all I need*, I heard God whisper to my spirit.

Honestly? I felt embarrassed. But I've walked with God long enough to know that obeying is better than second- (or twenty-second-) guessing His words or His ways. So I transferred my eleven dollars to Elise. Later I sent her another message letting her know that it was all I had at the time to give, but I offered it with my prayers that God would provide in ways that only He could.

Later, God brought another friend to mind who had posted something on social media asking if anyone had an urgent, pandemic-related need. Rather than give solely to a large national relief organization, this friend wanted to make a difference on a local, person-to-person level. I messaged this friend and told her about Elise's situation. I had no idea if she had already been flooded with needs, if she was still able to help. But the outcome wasn't up to me. The least I could do was be a possible bridge of connection.

Turns out, my friend who offered help was eager to give, and my friend who needed help was willing to accept it. I didn't know the details, but my heart was full at this glimpse of God's provision. He had heard our cries and He was faithful to answer.

Several weeks prior, I had invited a handful of friends in different locations and life stages to join me for a Be the Blessing Challenge. In the throes of writing this book, I told my friends the premise of the simple difference and asked them to spend one month committed to intentional kindness. Thirty days praying, *Lord, as I go on my way, have Your way with me*. At the end of that time, I sent out a response survey to learn how the challenge had impacted them. In addition to hearing about their experiences with showing kindness, I wanted to know how the challenge opened their eyes to seeing the kindness of God expressed through others in their own lives. To that end, one of the questions I asked was this: Did you receive any unexpected kindness during this time? If so, how did that affect you?

Elise was one of the friends who had taken my Be the Blessing Challenge. I never expected to read this answer to my question. Elise wrote,

---

One of my favorite gifts I have ever received was the $11 you sent me along with your friendship and words of love. It was completely unexpected, and I am completely serious. Because it was not only a gift of your everything, your tangible love, and physical support—it was also a powerful affirmation and fresh realization that my "small acts of kindness" matter to others. That being seen and known and loved can be communicated through "loaves and fishes." That God works through everything we offer for Him to use. It was truth you gifted me, really. Truth about how God feels and views our offerings. I can't put into words the profound freedom He gave me through your gift.

You may know that by telling your friend about my situation she gifted me $400. Which was a HUGE, huge, life-changing gift that allowed me to do things I no longer had the money to do . . . like buy more contacts instead of going through my day caring for everyone in my home legally blind. And I am so, so moved and grateful for her gift!! She literally put food in my children's mouths.

BUT—your gift went straight to my heart. I can hear Jesus's tone better as He watched different sizes of gifts being given at the temple. The truth is that our all ALWAYS has a huge impact in the kingdom of God. And, more importantly, our gift of all always impacts the heart of our King. He is not unaffected by His children's kindness to one another.

Your gift helped me get up, get my chin up, get my eyes up, and say, "Okay, Lord! If You entrust even a tiny seed to me, I'll plant it. Put anything 'small' in my hands and I won't be afraid or ashamed to use it because it's 'all' I have. I'm reminded how You can usher in joy, peace, and freedom by Your truth into a life with small kindnesses."

———

Reading Elise's response left me speechless. I didn't have four hundred dollars to give like my other friend. But that's not what God asked of me. All I had was eleven bucks, which was nothing in my eyes, meaningless in my economic impact calculations. But I knew the Lord wanted me to give my all, regardless of how I sized up or esteemed the gift. Never in my wildest dreams would I have guessed that my measly offering would mean so much to my dear friend. Yet, again, God taught me and Elise—a shared lesson from different viewpoints—that He alone is responsible for the impact we make and the outcome-shape our kindness takes.

The story Elise referenced of Jesus watching gifts given at the temple is a good one for us to consider as we think about giving our not-enough.

Jesus sat down near the collection box in the Temple and watched as the crowds dropped in their money. Many rich people put in large amounts. Then a poor widow came and dropped in two small coins.

Jesus called his disciples to him and said, "I tell you the truth, this poor widow has given more than all the others who are making contributions. For they gave a tiny part of their surplus, but she, poor as she is, has given everything she had to live on."[9]

There's so much in these five short sentences. First, I wonder if Jesus wasn't the only person keeping a watchful eye on the collection box. Perhaps seats near the offering box were prized. The fact that Jesus drew specific attention to the widow's gift makes me think that other people had their attention fixed on the large gift givers. Perhaps ears perked up when a deluge of coins poured into the collection box, the fast and furious clink of metal on metal a signal of the giver's religious piety and prestige. In the same way, maybe listening ears were followed by darting eyes when the steady stream of money was replaced with two barely audible clinks.

Then I wonder how the widow felt giving her two-coin gift. Was she ashamed she didn't have more to offer the Lord? Was she afraid that giving all she had would leave her hungry and homeless? Was she hopeful God would honor her sacrifice? Confident? Humble? Fearful? Discouraged? The text doesn't say. But this we do know: Jesus esteemed her gift. Regardless of how she felt about it or what onlookers in the temple thought about it, God called out the value of giving her all.

Two coins. Eleven dollars. Five loaves. One shovel. Let God take your not-enough and multiply it into abundance.

## THREE KEYS TO LIVING
### *the simple difference*

**Pray it bold.**

*God, thank You for being the One who can see the whole picture and who can multiply the meager. What I have to give often feels like simply not enough. Change the way I see. Help me to focus on Your power and not my own resources. I want to give my all—I trust that You can use it to do more than I could even imagine. Show Your power through my simple offerings. Amen.*

**Live it now.**

- When a need feels too big to meet and you're tempted to do nothing, just give exactly what you have.
- Look for a way to be a connector. You may not have the resources to help but you might know someone who does.
- Don't let shame shackle you into believing God can't use you. Write down Ephesians 3:20 and read it daily.

**Say it loud.**

God can transform my not-enough into abundance.

*twelve*

# it's not about you

In our exploration of how our small, ordinary acts of deliberate kindness can make a big difference, there's something I want to make sure I've said loud and clear: it's not about us.

I do not want you to get to the end of this book with a resolve to simply do more or try harder. If you're focused on hustling enough to be kind enough, you've missed the point. Does living the simple difference take action and intention on our part? Absolutely. But it also takes a surrendered heart. Which leads to a question I've been chewing on for quite some time. I can't get it out of my head. It goes like this:

What if the display of God's power in our lives is directly related to acknowledging our need for Him?

I've seen the evidence play out more times than I can count. For almost a decade I've watched a friend desperately try to grow her family. Every avenue explored, every expense exhausted. A child briefly placed in her arms, only to be taken. So much unbearable heartache. Yet my friend demonstrated an ongoing surrender to God's goodness in the shape of suffering and sorrow. Last week she welcomed a child into their forever family. Only God.

Another friend was recently faced with a weighty decision without a clear answer. There would be lasting implications, no matter which outcome won out. She couldn't reason through it on her own. In her wrestling, God put the image of a person in her mind whom she needed to connect with. But she didn't know this woman. I wasn't aware of any of this, yet I felt compelled to connect my friend who was wrestling with another friend who had walked a similar road. Can you guess? The woman my friend needed to talk to was the one I introduced her to. Only God.

A couple sat on our living room couch late one night and asked if they could tell us their story. My husband and I leaned in. I couldn't have guessed the brand of struggle, sin, and despair their marriage had gone through. Nor could I have imagined the story of healing and redemption they're now living. "As long as you're breathing, there is hope," they said. My husband and I weren't personally in crisis, but I knew these words were true and timely beyond seasons of despair. I tucked them into my heart. Hope in hopeless situations—only with God.

Not one of these friends would have chosen their circumstances. But in their greatest need, they each experienced God's kindness and great power in a very personal way. That is a gift not one of them would trade.

We've touched on many small dilemmas and sizable needs throughout this book. We're all keenly aware of the seemingly too-big-to-fix problems that weigh down society and break our hearts.

I wish I could reach through these pages and listen to the unexpected, undesirable, hope-unraveling circumstances you're currently living through. We've all got something. But in my lack of knowing,

God knows. He sees you. He is with you. And I'm wondering if He's prompting all of us to stop and ask: What if the display of God's power in my life is directly related to acknowledging my need for Him?

What if I can't be part of creating a tidal wave of positive change until I positively grasp how much I need God to do it?

In other words: Need Him big = See Him BIG.

If I'm honest, my most human response is that I don't want to need God. On the surface it seems easier to be competent and self-sufficient. I want life to be easy and comfortable enough that I can keep things rolling smoothly by my own try-hard grit. Or when the rubber meets the road and I start smelling that awful scent of tire burning, I still want to be able to speed up or slow down or course correct on my own. But that kind of life only yields more of me. And that's really *not* what I want.

I really want more of God.

I want to see Him work powerfully and move mightily. I want that for my family and friends. I want that for you.

• • •

In the midst of personal crisis, national unrest, or a global pandemic, people ask, "Where is God?" Here's what I'm coming to believe more than ever: He's in our need. He's in our lack. He's present and powerful when we're ready to admit how desperate we are without Him.

I recently finished reading *The Hiding Place* by Corrie ten Boom, the classic true story of a heroic Dutch watchmaker who shared the light of the gospel through the darkest hours of World War II. She saved lives by opening her home and making secret compartments to hide Jews, sharing the not-enough of what she had, and even scooting over to make more room in her own flea-infested bed. The ripples of her kindness were unimaginably wide. I wept at the horror of people being hunted down, imprisoned in unfathomable conditions, and slaughtered. I also wept at the unwavering hope one middle-aged woman lived and the impact it made on others.

Corrie saw with stark clarity what I'm just beginning to realize: "Perhaps only when human effort had done its best and failed, would God's power alone be free to work."[1]

Corrie tried every way within her power to keep the people in her care safe and protected. You'll have to read *The Hiding Place* to learn all the brave and brutal details. But I can tell you that ultimately her human effort wasn't enough. But God's was.

I believe the end of our rope is the beginning of God's grace. This is true in our individual circumstances and in our desire to make this world a better place. Mother Teresa said, "I alone cannot change the world, but I can cast a stone across the waters to create many ripples."[2]

Indeed it will take a collective of individuals—you and me and every other person willing to be a simple difference maker—in order to change the world beyond our personal spheres. But Mother Teresa's words are also accurate in that alone—on our own, by our own power—we cannot do-good-hustle or strong-arm the world into lasting change. We cannot even guarantee our kindness will make a single ripple when cast into a sea of people—it might just sink like a rock with little notice.

It is God's power that moves the water.

I can't help but think of the famous story of how God used one small stone to create mighty waves of change. I'm thinking of the rock that took down a mighty giant. You're probably familiar with the Bible story of David and Goliath. (If not, you can find it in 1 Samuel 17.) Goliath was the nearly ten-foot-tall Philistine warrior who threatened to destroy the Israelite army. Day after day, for forty days, Goliath came forward and challenged any man from the opposing side who had enough guts to face him. The future of both nations rested on this single man-to-man battle. Whichever side was victorious would get their enemy's land, wealth, and surviving citizens. Saul was king of Israel at the time, and not one soldier in his mighty legion was willing to fight such a powerful opponent with everything on the line.

The Israelites were woefully aware of their insufficiency, but they failed to understand that God's power was what they really needed. Enter David. David was a young shepherd and the youngest of eight sons; his father sent him to the battlefield to bring provisions to his brothers. When David got to the front lines and heard about the dire situation his people faced, he didn't hesitate to offer his help.

What made the young shepherd willing to face an opponent that hundreds of grown men trained in combat wouldn't? Was it because David was simply conceited, like his older brother suggested? Did he think so highly of himself that he believed he could accomplish what no one else could? I don't think so.

David's uncanny courage came from knowing that it would be *God's* power that would defeat the giant. And he was willing to be the conduit.

Without a breastplate or sword or spear, David approached Goliath with nothing but a sling and pouch full of river rocks. He took one smooth stone, placed it in his sling, and let it soar. The rock sank into the Philistine's forehead, taking down the ostensibly unconquerable soldier.

A sheep-tending little brother stood victorious on the battlefield, showing God's undeniable power.

So what does an old Bible story that reads more like a mythic fairy tale have to do with living the simple difference? While it's unlikely that you or I will ever be asked to save a nation by slaying an epic giant, we each are destined to face opportunities to help when the odds are stacked against us. Surely we will see someone in need and look down at our own measly stones and be tempted to think, *It's impossible for someone like me to make a difference.*

The right response is, Yeah, it is impossible—without God. But with God, all things are possible.

David wasn't responsible for the outcome. He was responsible for hearing God, responding in faith, and showing up. An entire nation of people was changed because of it.

We offer our pebble. God's power magnifies the ripples. He accomplishes with a simple stone what we cannot do on our own.

• • •

Those ripples of change won't happen unless we're willing to give God our not-enough with hopeful expectation that He'll make it more than we could imagine.

Sometimes what feels most lacking in our lives isn't money, like it was in my story about wanting to help my friend Elise. Though I often wish I had a greater financial capacity to give, there's another limited resource that holds the key to kindness, the key to making a big impact. And it always seems to be in short supply in my life. I'm talking about time.

Doing all the simple difference things we've talked about hinges on having time to do it. Am I right?

It takes time to listen, time to pray, time to speak up, time to show love and compassion to a neighbor. Sometimes I feel hostage to God's twenty-four-hour cycle. Can't He give us just a little extra wiggle room? There are so many good things I want to do. If only I could turn the clock hands back with a magical device, a la Hermione Granger, I'd be able to double my impact in the world! Or at least be able to run to the grocery store, pick up the kids from baseball practice, meet a deadline, fix dinner, and have enough time to volunteer at the youth center or make soup for a sick friend. Do these kinds of thoughts ever cross your mind too?

Not enough time is my number one excuse (read: sometimes totally valid reason and sometimes the myth I hide behind) for opting out of pursuing a life of intentional kindness. Not that I want to be intentionally rude or unkind, of course. I'm sure that's not your MO either. But let's peel off another layer of our collective self-protective, self-reliant mask, shall we?

Our natural tendency is to look at our finite resource of time and then consider how much our own needs and wants will require. If you're anything like me, more often than not there's not much left over. And what is left over—measly minutes and the occasional haphazard hour—feels as useful as the dry crust from a toddler's peanut butter sandwich. The child has chosen the bulk of what was available to him and called it good. The rest was cast off. Discarded as useless. But what's true of unwanted bites of bread is also true of leftover bits of time—it still has value. The crust is still nutritious; it can still nourish a body.

In the same way, what if the bits and pieces of our time held value for a life marked by kindness? This circles back again to the opening premise that the simple difference is lived less by going out of our way and more by surrendering to the Spirit's leading as we simply go about our day. Praying, *Lord, as I go on my way, have Your way with me.*

Here's the point: stop using time as an excuse. Do you find yourself thinking or saying things like, "I'd really like to love and serve others, but I have a job and people who need me, plus some dreams and desires I'd rather not put on the back burner"? If this is a repeated reason why you can't live eyes wide open to the people beyond your four walls or close circle, then it's time for you to join me in reframing the way we think about how God can use our time.

If God can multiply loaves and fish, surely He can expand the impact of finite hours and leftover minutes.

Let me give you an ordinary example from my friend Audra. She took my Be the Blessing Challenge and shared with me about how God worked through the limits of her time to meet the needs of another. Audra wrote,

———

On a Monday afternoon, I dropped the kids off at a friend's house for a swap. It was my turn to have a couple hours on my own. My mind raced as I drove home in a quiet car about what to do with my "free time." The first thought I had was to tackle the mound of clean laundry piled on the couch. As I began to fold, I also began to pray (these things are easier to do with a quiet house). As I prayed, my friend Angela came to mind. Her family had been sick with the flu for weeks. After praying for their healing, I felt a nudge to send a check-in text. After the text I felt another nudge to offer dinner. She gladly accepted my offer for dinner.

At first I wondered if I could pull off making and delivering dinner within my allotted "free time." But I decided I could pick up Plaza Produce since we had a gift card. So I quickly put the clean laundry away (the dirty dishes would have to wait) and picked up dinner for my friend and her family. Five smiling faces and waving arms greeted me through their front window as I approached their home. Her children were full of excitement as I left their food on the front porch. Their joy was contagious, and I smiled wide as I drove home.

The blessing of giving a simple meal filled me, washing away the anxiety I felt about my own "to-do" list. How easy it would have been to ignore the nudge to offer dinner, but it felt like God was the one offering encouragement to my friend and I'm thankful I got to be part of it.

———

I love this simple story of a woman who let God multiply the impact of her time. I have known that racing-mind feeling Audra described when faced with what to do with limited alone time. Quick, be ultra-productive, do all the chores you're behind on and get ahead on the ones about to pile up, plus try to rest, relax, and do something fun just for yourself—and do it all in two hours. (And all the mothers nod along.)

No one would fault Audra for praying for her sick friend and then moving right along. There's certainly nothing wrong with taking care of your own family, self, or responsibilities.

But Audra approached her small pocket of open time with a heart surrendered to God. She was willing to let Him use her limited resources in whatever way He saw fit. She was keenly aware of her own needs—laundry to fold, dirty dishes to wash, a tired soul to tend to—yet she was also mindful of the needs of her friend. By responding with a simple prayer, a text, and picking up takeout, she was able to see God's compassion at work.

Yes, needing Him big equals seeing Him big.

On an ordinary Monday night, a tired mom named Audra saw God big—and her simple kindness helped her friend Angela and her children see Him too.

On an extraordinary day long ago, a sheep-tending boy named David saw God big—and his courage changed the trajectory of history for his people.

How will you see God today? How will you respond to the big and little needs around you? Will you be disheartened by your small stones and inadequate stature? Or will you choose a posture that recognizes God's power? Will you live expectantly surrendered to the Spirit's leading? Will you be ready to *be the blessing*?

Today and every day, you get to open your eyes, smile wide, give freely, love boldly, choose mercy. As you go to the chiropractor or visit your grandma, as you fill up your gas tank or ride the subway, as you pick up your dry cleaning, sit on the sidelines, or wait for your coffee, you can look for opportunities to make a difference.

Today you get to offer your pebble of love and compassion and trust God to create lasting ripples.

Together our simple, consistent, intentional acts of courageous kindness can create waves of change.

Let's be people who acknowledge our great need for God, so through our lives His greatness can be seen.

## *the simple difference*

**Pray it bold.**

*God, thank You for choosing to use the small stones and small moments of my life. I recognize that making a difference isn't about me. It's about Your power and goodness. I'm willing to be a conduit. I give You my time, my money, and my voice. I give You my smile, my hands, and my feet. Help me to love people—all messy and messed up—like You love them, with endless kindness and compassion. The needs around me are so big, but You are bigger. Help us all to see more of You today. Amen.*

**Live it now.**

- When the odds are stacked against you, remember whose power you can trust in.
- Don't discount the difference offering the bits and pieces of your time can make.
- As you do your daily tasks—like folding laundry or picking up a prescription—ask God to show you someone who needs a reminder of His kindness.

**Say it loud.**

I will offer my pebble and trust God's power to magnify the ripples.

# *acknowledgments*

To my husband, Chris, thank you for teaching me to be where my feet are and supporting the writing of this book in a thousand ways. I couldn't do this without you.

To my three amazing sons, Noah, Elias, and Jude, you are forever my greatest treasures and my favorite teachers. I love watching you grow. Keep shaping the world with your love, your kindness, your silliness, and your strength. Thanks for cheering me on.

To Elise, thank you for continually pointing to the kindness of God—in your life, in my life, and through the pages of Scripture. Your friendship is one of His most lavish gifts to me.

To Mindy, Anjuli, Tracey, Desiree, Aliza, Sara, Kimberlee, and Kyan, thank you for being my people, for receiving my tears, making me laugh, and lifting me up on the wings of your prayers. I'm forever grateful for the ways Voxer, morning walks, and evening porch dates have continued to knit our hearts together. Your kindness and encouragement have made all the difference.

To the (in)courage staff, Anna, Grace, and Joy, I'll never get over the gift it is to do the work we do. Partnering with three of the most talented, wise, and generous women I know is God's kindness upon kindness.

To the (in)courage writers, thank you for teaching me what it means to show up fully, love deeply, share beautifully gritty stories, and continually point to the hope of Christ. You are the difference makers!

To the incredible Revell team, especially Rachel, Robin, and Eileen, thank you for believing in this book and supporting it every step of the way with your great skill and enthusiasm. What a profound privilege to bring meaningful words into the world together.

To Audra, Beth, Esther, Kathy, Lisa and David, May, Michele, and every other named and unnamed person whose story spilled over into these pages, you inspire me! I am a better person and I see the goodness of God more clearly because of your example. Ripple upon ripple. Your stones of kindness are creating waves of change.

And to you, my reader, thank you for taking this journey with me. My hope is that these pages have sparked new ideas, fresh reflection, and deeper conviction about the countless small, intentional, consistent ways you can impact the world right where you are with exactly what you have. But above all, I pray you have encountered the kindness of God. That you see more clearly how God goes to unimaginable lengths to demonstrate the power of His love for *you*. You are so loved, friend. Embrace that love and share it with others as you go on your way today.

And of course, to my Jesus. Where would I be without You? Thank You for revealing Your kindness to me with searing clarity through the process of writing this book, and for inviting us all to partner with You in loving this busted-up world. Thanks for not giving up on me—on us. Help us to use our daily stones well. I trust You to keep magnifying the ripples.

# notes

## Introduction: Be the Blessing

1. Luke 10:36 MSG.
2. Matt. 22:37, 39.

## Chapter One  Why Kindness

1. Fred Rogers, *You Are Special: Neighborly Wit and Wisdom from Mister Rogers* (New York: Penguin Books, 1995).
2. Christopher Klein, "8 Things You May Not Know about Jonas Salk and the Polio Vaccine," History.com, March 25, 2020, https://www.history.com/news/8-things-you-may-not-know-about-jonas-salk-and-the-polio-vaccine.
3. Rom. 5:8.
4. John 3:16 NLT.
5. Rom. 2:4 NLT.
6. John 13:34–35.
7. 1 John 4:19.
8. Gen. 1:27.

## Chapter Two  Embrace the Awkward

1. "Beth Moore: The Hair Brush (LIFE Today / James Robison)," YouTube video, 8:24, posted by "lifetodaytv," September 10, 2020, https://www.youtube.com/watch?v=Xtk5WgzZcYA.
2. "Beth Moore: The Hair Brush," YouTube video, 0:30–0:35.
3. Stephen D. Renn, *Expository Dictionary of Bible Words: Word Studies for Key English Bible Words Based on the Hebrew and Greek Texts* (Peabody, MA: Hendrickson Publishers, 2005).
4. Darrel L. Bock, *Luke: The NIV Application Commentary* (Grand Rapids: Zondervan, 1996).
5. Luke 10:33.

6. J. D. Douglas, Merrill C. Tenney, and Moisés Silva, *Zondervan Illustrated Bible Dictionary* (Grand Rapids: Zondervan, 2011).

7. Renn, *Expository Dictionary of Bible Words*.

8. Luke 10:34–35.

9. Luke 10:36–37.

## Chapter Three  Every Word Counts

1. Michele Cushatt, "The Words Those Who Suffer Need to Hear the Most," October 5, 2018, (in)courage, https://www.incourage.me/2018/10/the-words-those-who-suffer-need-to-hear-most.html.

2. Col. 3:12.

3. Col. 3:12.

4. 1 John 4:19.

## Chapter Four  Not Your Last Resort

1. 1 Tim. 2:1, emphasis mine.

2. Phil. 4:6.

3. Luke 5:16.

4. Luke 18:1, emphasis mine.

5. 1 Thess. 5:16–18.

6. Heb. 4:16.

7. Matt. 18:20.

8. May Patterson, "Pray with Strangers–Even If You Don't Really Want To," May Patterson, updated February 9, 2020, https://maypatterson.com/2020/02/pray-with-strangers-even-if-you-dont-really-want-to/.

9. John 8:1–11.

10. Luke 19:1–10 MSG.

11. *Zéteó*, Thayer's Greek Lexicon, BibleHub, accessed February 19, 2021, https://biblehub.com/greek/2212.htm.

12. *Sózó*, Strong's Concordance, BibleHub, accessed February 19, 2021, https://biblehub.com/greek/4982.htm.

## Chapter Five  Hardest at Home

1. Becky Keife, *No Better Mom for the Job: Parenting with Confidence (Even When You Don't Feel Cut Out for It)* (Bloomington, MN: Bethany House, 2019).

2. 1 Cor. 13:1–3 NLT.

3. Gal. 6:9–10 MSG.

4. 1 Pet. 3:8–9 MSG.

5. 1 Cor. 13:4–7 NLT.

6. Good News Movement, via @keon_richkid, June 24, 2020, Instagram video, https://www.instagram.com/p/CB1DfxsgJeo/.

7. AndyStanley, Twitter post, April 17, 2013, https://twitter.com/AndyStanley/status/324713440541290498.

## Chapter Six  Kindness in Crisis

1. Col. 1:17.

2. Fred Rogers, Goodreads, accessed February 19, 2021, https://www.goodreads.com/quotes/198594-when-i-was-a-boy-and-i-would-see-scary.

3. "Green. Yellow. Red. Quarantined Neighbors Looking after Each Other with Window Message," Click on Detroit, April 1, 2020, https://www.clickondetroit.com/news/world /2020/04/01/green-yellow-red-quarantined-neighbors-looking-after-each-other-with -window-message/.

4. Mitchel Summers, "Winfield Residents Play Tic-Tac-Toe with Senior Citizens," 13*WIBW*, March 27, 2020, https://www.wibw.com/content/news/Winfield-residents -play-Tic-Tac-Toe-with-Senior-Citizens-569164991.html.

5. Mic. 6:8 ESV.

6. John 16:33.

7. 2 Tim. 1:7.

## Chapter Seven  Undeserved

1. Luke 15:11–32.

2. Rom. 2:4 NLT.

## Chapter Eight  Where Your Feet Are

1. Phil. 2:3–4.

2. Phil. 2:5.

3. Phil. 2:6–8.

4. John 15:13.

5. 1 John 3:16.

## Chapter Nine  In It for the Long Haul

1. Luke 10:39–42.

2. John 11:1–35.

3. Rom. 12:15.

4. John 11:36.

5. John 13:34–35.

6. John 11:39.

7. John 11:39–43.

## Chapter Ten  Unexpected Teachers

1. Jennifer McClellan, "One Third of Middle- and High-Schoolers Were Bullied Last Year, Study Shows," *USA Today*, September 24, 2018, https://www.usatoday.com/story /life/allthemoms/2018/09/24/one-out-three-students-were-bullied-us-school-last-year /1374631002/.

2. Lisa Leonard, *Brave Love: Making Space for You to Be You* (Grand Rapids: Zondervan, 2019), 124–25.

3. Ana Rivera, "Young Girl's Kind Gesture to Help Oxford Walmart Employee Sparks Unlikely Friendship," *ABC7NY*, June 19, 2020, https://abc7ny.com/society/little-girl-goes -out-of-her-way-to-help-walmart-employee/6256086/; Goodable, Twitter post, June 19, 2020, https://twitter.com/Goodable/status/1274067959036641286/photo/1.

## Chapter Eleven  Giving Your Not-Enough

1. Ps. 31:14–15 CSB.

2. Ps. 103:2 NLT.

3. Matt. 17:17–18 MSG.

4. Matt. 17:20 MSG.

5. Eph. 3:16–17, emphases mine.
6. Eph. 3:17–19.
7. Eph. 3:20, emphases mine.
8. John 6:1–13.
9. Mark 12:41–44 NLT.

## Chapter Twelve  It's Not about You

1. Corrie ten Boom with Elizabeth and John Sherrill, *The Hiding Place*, 35th anniversary ed. (Grand Rapids: Chosen, 2006), 138.
2. Mother Teresa, GoodReads, accessed December 7, 2020, https://www.goodreads.com/quotes/49502-i-alone-cannot-change-the-world-but-i-can-cast.

**Becky Keife** is the community manager for DaySpring's (in)courage, a widely followed online community. Through the power of shared stories and meaningful Bible-based resources, (in)courage helps women build community, celebrate diversity, and become women of courage.

Becky is also a popular speaker and is the author of *No Better Mom for the Job: Parenting with Confidence (Even When You Don't Feel Cut Out for It)* and the Bible study *Courageous Kindness: Live the Simple Difference Right Where You Are*. Becky is a huge fan of Voxer, Sunday naps, and anything with cinnamon. She and her husband live near Los Angeles, where they enjoy hiking sunny trails with their three spirited sons. Connect with Becky on Instagram @beckykeife or at beckykeife.com.

# Discover More Books
# by Becky Keife

If you loved *The Simple Difference* and want to dive deeper into what Scripture teaches about making a meaningful impact right where you are, then you'll love the *Courageous Kindness* Bible study from Becky Keife and the (in)courage community, as well as *No Better Mom for the Job*.

To book Becky as a speaker for your next event, visit

# beckykeife.com/speaking

# Bible Studies to Empower Your Life

In these six-week Bible studies, your friends at (in)courage will help you dive deep into real-life issues, the transforming power of God's Word, and what it means to courageously live your faith.

# 100 Days of Hope and Assurance

In this 100-day devotional, the (in)courage community reaches into the grief and pain of both crisis and ordinary life. Each day includes a key Scripture, a heartening devotion, and a prayer to remind you that God is near and hope is possible. You won't find tidy bows or trite quick fixes, just arrows pointing you straight to Jesus.

# (in)courage is an online community where
women gather to build community, celebrate diversity, and become women of courage. Founded in 2009 by DaySpring, the Christian products subsidiary of Hallmark Cards, Inc., (in)courage is like a virtual living room where every day one of thirty writers takes a turn sharing a story of what Jesus looks like in her life. Together we link arms as God's daughters and lean on one another for wisdom, strength, and insight beyond our own experience. (in)courage also creates Bible studies and devotionals to help women grow in their faith!

Join us at **www.incourage.me**
& connect with us on social media!